T0090499

Also by Qaiser Abbas

- Tick Tick Dollar (International bestseller)
- Made in Crises
- Power of Teams
- Leadership Insights

Speed
Coaching

Leaders' Playbook for Creating a Culture of
Impactful Coaching Conversations

Qaiser Abbas

Award-winning Leadership Coach
Author of International Bestseller, Tick Tick Dollar

BALBOA.PRESS
A DIVISION OF HAY HOUSE

Balboa Press books may be ordered through booksellers or by contacting:

Balboa Press
A Division of Hay House
1663 Liberty Drive
Bloomington, IN 47403
www.balboapress.com
844-682-1282

Because of the dynamic nature of the Internet, any web addresses or links contained in this book may have changed since publication and may no longer be valid. The views expressed in this work are solely those of the author and do not necessarily reflect the views of the publisher, and the publisher hereby disclaims any responsibility for them.

The author of this book does not dispense medical advice or prescribe the use of any technique as a form of treatment for physical, emotional, or medical problems without the advice of a physician, either directly or indirectly. The intent of the author is only to offer information of a general nature to help you in your quest for emotional and spiritual well-being. In the event you use any of the information in this book for yourself, which is your constitutional right, the author and the publisher assume no responsibility for your actions.

Any people depicted in stock imagery provided by Getty Images are models, and such images are being used for illustrative purposes only.
Certain stock imagery © Getty Images.

Print information available on the last page.

ISBN: 979-8-7652-4409-8 (sc)
ISBN: 979-8-7652-4410-4 (e)

Balboa Press rev. date: 12/20/2023

All author's proceeds will go to **Possibilities Foundation** to educate out-of-school, underprivileged children and support the **'My First Bike'** movement, aiming to provide 100,000 deprived children (7-12 years old) their life's first ever bicycle through a well-designed, fun-filled, and memorable team-building/ leadership development learning experience by Qaiser Abbas and his team of over 250 leadership trainers and coaches.

"Ultimately, leaders' job is to prepare future leadership. Speed Coaching offers the ideas, tools, and actions that enable leaders to have positive conversations that help their employees grow. The best coaching occurs less in formal settings and more in informal conversations."

– **Dave Ulrich** - Father of modern HR. Rensis Likert Professor, Ross School of Business, University of Michigan. Partner, The RBL Group

"Speed Coaching" is a useful dialogue for any manager or leader wishing to challenge their own style and approach. The modern workplace demands that we learn and develop skills quickly, and on the job, rather than taking valuable time out for more structured/costly training. Qaiser's book can really support that whole process, and I wish him every success with it. –

– **Julie Starr** - author of The Coaching Manual, The Mentoring Manual, and Brilliant Coaching.

"Speed Coaching" is a game-changer for leaders and managers looking to create a coaching culture within their organization. Drawing from his extensive experience as a leadership coach, Qaiser presents a practical and research-based framework that is easy to understand and implement. I highly recommend this book to anyone looking to improve their leadership skills and build stronger relationships with their team."

– **Will Linssen** - #1 Leadership Coach (Global Gurus 2022) and CEO, Global Coach Group

Speed Coaching will empower you to nurture the collaborative spirit at your workplace and gain confidence in engaging your team to achieve meaningful growth.

– **Dr. Marshall Goldsmith,** Thinkers50 Hall of Fame

Author of New York Times Bestsellers *'What Got you Here, Won't Get You There,'* "Speed Coaching" is a must-read for anyone looking to institute coaching as part of their organization's culture. Qaiser Abbas has magnificently broken down complex coaching concepts into an easy-to-apply conversational framework that leaders can practice in everyday interactions with their teams. Speed Coaching is a testament to Qaiser Abbas's skill as a coach and his commitment to helping organizations worldwide transform through coaching."

– **Chip Conley** - New York Times Best Selling Author. Founder, Modern Elder Academy. Former Head of Hospitality and Strategy at Airbnb

"Qaiser's Speed Coaching is a one-of-a-kind leading-edge book. Definitely a must-read for anyone who is in a leadership or management position. In today's world, it is essential to develop practical new skill sets in communication to engage and retain employees and co-workers. Qaiser delivers simple, practical techniques for increasing productivity and motivation to produce great results. The group interaction is based on human behavioral and psychological techniques that actually work, leading to the formation of a team of confident individuals who are encouraged to take initiative with open enjoyment. Well done Qaiser!"

– **Yvonne Oswald Ph.D.** - Best-selling, award-winning author of Every Word has Power, *(now in eleven languages)*

"We live in a world where communication is often bite-sized and leaders have precious few moments to support their people as allies in helping them take smart next steps with ownership for follow through. Speed Coaching is great tool for doing just that."

– **Peter Bregman** - #1 Executive Coach. Bestselling author of 18 Minutes and Leading with Emotional Courage

"If you are a leader, a coach, or a human who wants to learn a new technique to gain more clarity in any situation, then this book is for you. Qaiser shows you the WHY and HOW after changing your mindset to use Speed Coaching as a tool, technique, or a new way of life to unleash your full potential."

– **Abdallah Aljurf** - Founder of ICF Saudi Arabia Chapter, Leadership Development Consultant

This groundbreaking book is filled with practical tools, real-world examples, and research-backed strategies, all woven together with Qaiser's unique storytelling prowess. Qaiser masterfully distills complex coaching concepts into easily digestible, actionable insights, making them accessible for anyone to implement and benefit from. I wholeheartedly endorse "Speed Coaching" and urge anyone aspiring to elevate their leadership skills to immerse themselves in its pages. Don't miss this rare opportunity to learn from a true visionary like Qaiser Abbas, whose passion, expertise, and wisdom are guaranteed to leave an indelible impact on your life and career.

– **Arif Anis** - USA Today & Wall Street Journal Bestselling Author

To my elder brother and role model

Dr. Jawaz Jaffari

Thank you for being my earliest inspiration to dream big dreams. With your personal example, you taught me to take full responsibility for my life and to find my own path amidst fierce challenges and endless crises.

Whatever I am today, it is because of your continued support and challenge. You are the reason that every single day I commit to being the very best I can be.

CONTENTS

Foreword 1

About The Book 5

A Guided Tour to Speed Coaching................................13

PART 01 – SPEED COACHING CONCEPTS

Chapter 01 – Why Speed Coaching?...................................21

Chapter 02 – Speed Coaching Fundamentals for Leaders ...34

PART 02 – SPEED COACHING SKILLS

Stage #1 - LEARN – The Basics of Speed Coaching 49

Chapter 03 – The Mindset of a Coach-Like Leader 51

Chapter 04 – Focus of a Coaching Leader 69

Stage #2 - EXPERIMENT – With Speed Coaching Skills.............87

Chapter 05 – Speed Coaching Formula 89

Chapter 06 – Core Coaching Skills to Speed Coach 102

Stage #3 - APPLY – Coaching Frameworks at the Workplace........131

Chapter 07 – Framework for Coaching Conversations......133

Chapter 08 – Pillars of a Coaching Relationship..............146

Stage #4 - PRACTICE – Speed Coaching as a Way of Life 185

Chapter 09 – The Transition from Bossing to Coaching...187

Chapter 10 – Overcoming Speed Coaching Barriers 195

PART 03 – SPEED COACHING CULTURE

Chapter 11 – Seeding a Speed Coaching Culture..............205

Chapter 12 – Nurturing a Speed Coaching Culture
(Process & Tools) 213

Chapter 13 – How do Coaching & Routine
Conversations Differ? 228

Chapter 14 – Speed Coaching in Action 235

References 247

Acknowledgments 257

FOREWORD

DR. MARSHALL GOLDSMITH

Speed Coaching is a fresh concept in leadership coaching. This incredible masterpiece from Qaiser will change the way you view managerial coaching and help you support your team in the way they need to succeed. The concepts, models, tools, and framework presented in *Speed Coaching* are original, tested, practical, and completely hands-on.

Qaiser's work on coaching has always inspired me enormously. His coaching style is compelling and has helped countless leaders improve their team interactions to create positive, lasting change.

Very skillfully, Qaiser has condensed the fundamentals of coaching into a few core ideas. *Speed Coaching* will enable you to extend growth-oriented support to your employees without making them feel formally "coached" — making them more receptive and you less burdened to spend scheduled hours in your office with them. What differentiates *Speed Coaching* from other books on coaching is that it offers valuable and powerful ways of implementing coaching into everyday conversations with the people who rely most on their leader's support.

The fact is, gone are the days when the recipe for building a great career was simple. Building technical expertise and becoming good at your work used to be enough. Doing your job well meant having the right answers. If you could prove yourself through your great work, you would rise the ladder and eventually move to higher management. A manager's job was to ensure that subordinates had those same answers. The goal was to direct and develop employees who understood how the business worked and was able to reproduce its previous successes.

However, this is no longer applicable. Rapid, constant, and disruptive change is now the norm, and what succeeded in the past is no longer a guide to what will succeed in the future. Leaders often recognize this fact. Unfortunately, the challenge of how they help their team to develop professionally is often lost and becomes a low priority in the bustle of business life.

Qaiser's *Speed Coaching* is an eye-opener for leaders. The book clarifies that 21st-century managers should not spend hours talking to their team members to provide them with some hour-long formal coaching sessions. Instead, the best coaching is hands-on, engaged, and occurs naturally through employee conversations.

Leaders must inspire fresh energy, innovation, and commitment and challenge their teams to adapt to constantly changing environments.

Managers must avoid getting stuck in the past, focusing on performance management instead of developing performance. They must see employees as a portfolio of talent in which they invest time and energy, as a way of investing in a company. Through coaching, leaders help each employee focus on developing those capabilities that will contribute most to individual and organizational success.

Employee retention is more crucial than ever. After all, people make an organization in the modern world. Qaiser advocates that to achieve critical results and remain competitive; you must see coaching not only as a means to shape individual performance but also as a means to build broader organizational capacity.

Employees are looking to be coached in a way that grows them, develops their strengths, and keeps them challenged at a company. This means managers can no longer sit in their offices, remain inaccessible, and pass on orders to their teams. Leaders are pushed to reinvent themselves to leverage their team and institution's creativity, energy, and learning in this new world.

Speed Coaching will engage you right from the first page to the finishing chapter, and it's relatable and real. Leaders who read this book will change how they interact with their teams.

Grounded in cutting-edge psychological principles and recent behavioral science, *Speed Coaching* is a must-read for leaders who want to create productive, engaged teams.

Speed Coaching will empower you to nurture the collaborative spirit at your workplace and gain confidence in engaging your team to achieve meaningful growth.

Dr. Marshall Goldsmith
Thinkers50 Hall of Fame
World's #1 Executive Coach
Author of New York Times Bestsellers *'What Got you Here, Won't Get You There,' 'Triggers,' 'Mojo,'* and *'The Earned Life'*

ABOUT THE BOOK

You don't have to be a certified coach to benefit from proven coaching tools and principles. *'Speed Coaching'* helps leaders make the best of what coaching offers - the dialogue, tools, and mindset to think like a coach, listen like a coach, talk like a coach, and act like a coach.

This book will help you learn how to spot and take advantage of daily opportunities to engage your teams in quick, focused, and meaningful coaching conversations, leveraging those interactions to transform yourself, your teams, and your organizations.

Instead of making coaching a structured, rigorous process offered to only a few key executives at the top, *'Speed Coaching'* aims to introduce coaching as an exchange of ideas and dialogues between employees and managers at all levels that is positive, motivating, and forward-looking.

Through *'Speed Coaching'* I intend to help leaders take advantage of the quick, often taken-for-granted conversations with their employees on a daily basis. The book will allow leaders to coach on-the-fly whenever the opportunity arises, taking a *sip* of the coaching process that is spontaneous, improvised, and powerful.

WHY ANOTHER BOOK ON COACHING?

Viewing the constraints of complicated, multi-step traditional coaching models, this quick read provides a fast and straightforward process that makes coaching memorable and accessible for novice and experienced leaders alike.

'Speed Coaching' is a substitute for formal coaching, which is usually time-consuming and sometimes gets overlooked for the more immediate responsibilities. The key is not to carve out time to coach but *embed coaching into the time you already have.*

WHAT MOTIVATED ME TO WRITE THIS BOOK?

Coaching doesn't have to be limited to the professional setting. Informal coaching conversations can take place anywhere and everywhere. Using the ATM Formula, you will soon learn in the book; you can convert almost every conversation into a coaching conversation.

Through *'Speed Coaching'*, we aim to create coach-like leaders who can turn everyday conversations into more insightful and result-oriented coaching dialogues.

'Speed Coaching' will make you ready and equipped to take advantage of a conversation during exchanges that happen every day – on an elevator, in the cafeteria, over an afternoon cup of coffee, or passing in the hallway. You will be able to contribute to creating a coaching culture where coaching becomes part of the organization's fabric.

WHAT IS SPEED COACHING?

Let me give you the simplest introduction to speed coaching.

Speed Coaching is an informal, usually unplanned or unexpected *opportunity* for a leader or a manager to have a dialogue with an employee aimed at facilitating the employee to *problem solve* or *learn from an experience.*

It is aimed at helping your teams to learn rather than instructing, directing, or teaching them. *'Speed Coaching'* is an informal communication process between two people that can be utilized in almost any context where the *Coachee* has a situation in which more than one solution is possible.

WHAT WILL YOU LEARN FROM THIS BOOK?

- You will see the difference between a 'unidirectional' conversation and a genuine dialogue: the power of using the language of coaching to achieve expectations, personal growth, and overall strategic success.
- With powerful, actionable coaching tools, you will learn to show up daily, knowing that what you say and do does make a difference.
- You will experience this new reality that everyone in an organization can master a new language called *'dialogue'* to improve leadership, result-focus, creativity, problem-solving, service excellence, and continuous learning.

'Speed Coaching' aims to equip you with hands-on coaching knowledge, skill, and practice. Grounded in deep research, experience, and practice, the book will improve your coaching dialogue skills.

HOW WILL SPEED COACHING BENEFIT YOUR BUSINESS?

In the last 12 years, helping leaders master the coaching leadership style has been my obsession. I have witnessed organizations transform when top leaders adopt *speed coaching* in their daily interactions.

It starts with the leadership teams in almost all cases, and then my team and I end up training everyone in the leadership roles in the entire organization through the science of speed coaching.

Over the years, we have done it with hundreds of leaders in dozens of organizations around the globe. In almost every case, within a few weeks of our interventions, everyone at all levels in the organization is spotted speaking the speed coaching language.

BENEFITS OF SPEED COACHING
Here are the most frequently reported benefits of using speed coaching leadership style:

- Organizations that embrace coaching as a preferred way of managing and leading experience higher performance and productivity. The exchange of meaningful and actionable feedback becomes the norm, not limited to annual performance appraisals. The willingness to share insights and ideas becomes accepted and expected at all levels - up, down, and across.
- Based on a simple, proven, and easy-to-use 'speed coaching framework' the leaders and managers at all levels in the organization start to engage their teams. It allows them to give feedback formally and informally, make agreements, set the

direction, and empower teams to take action with a sense of accountability.

- 'Speed Coaching' helps your organization create a 'coaching culture' based on understanding, collaboration, and growth principles. The constant follow-through on the ideas presented in the book will help your organization embody coaching as a usual way of life.

WHAT CAN LEADERS ACHIEVE THROUGH SPEED COACHING?

'Speed Coaching' will allow your leaders to embrace *a 'coach-like leadership style.'* They will be able to engage people in a positive exchange that enables the person to be coached, explore what is possible, and commit to constructive, forward-looking actions.

Using the simple four-step conversational framework, leaders can create mind-expanding conversations that leave the manager and employee feeling good about the interaction. *Speed Coaching* enables leaders to do the following:

- Discover what the employee is experiencing and understand their reality.
- Partner with them. Help them find solutions, think through options, and understand the implications.
- Commit to facilitating action and following up on progress, insights, and timing.

The conversations are spontaneous and flow naturally, suspending any judgment and skepticism and instilling self-motivation and commitment.

KEY QUESTIONS ADDRESSED IN THE BOOK:

- How to understand the coaching language?
- How to engage and excite your team using speed coaching?
- How to connect with your team better through coaching?
- How to co-create action plans with your people in a speed coaching style?
- How to gain commitment and ownership of results without pressure?

WHO IS THIS BOOK FOR?

In the last many years, I have helped professionals in various settings utilize *'Speed Coaching'* tools, frameworks, and methods. The audience who have benefitted the most from these concepts through my training interventions are the following:

- CEOs, Board Members, Directors
- C-Suit Executives, Business Leaders
- Entrepreneurs and Business owners
- Department Heads, Business Managers,
- Divisional Heads, Functional Heads
- General Managers, Senior Managers, Team Leaders
- Executive Coaches (both external and internal)
- Sports Coaches, Performance Coaches, Life Coaches
- Professional Corporate Trainers and Speakers
- Mentors who are tired of advising that people act upon
- HR Chiefs, Leaders, Directors, Heads

- Anyone who manages a team or has a supervisory role
- Teachers, Professors, Principals, Academic Heads
- Deans, HODs, and VCs of Universities
- Heads of Non-profit Organizations
- Religious Scholars & Speakers
- Government Officers at all levels
- Parents, & Family Heads

SPEED COACHING RESULTS:

 According to the research conducted by the Founder of Coaching, *Sir. John Whitmore,* coach-like leadership style produces the following results:

- Improved performance & productivity
- Greater employee engagement
- Improved job satisfaction & retention
- More time for the leader to focus on bigger goals
- Increased innovation
- Better use of people and knowledge
- People going the extra mile
- Greater agility and adaptability
- High-performance culture
- Enriched relationship between leader and team
- Life Skills for leaders
- Improved career development

"My main job is to produce results. If I sit in the office and coach my direct reports, who will ensure results?"
A manager's typical excuse for not coaching their teams

Whatever your excuse is for not being able to coach your team more frequently, this book is going to eliminate every justification of yours. The book will allow you to use coaching to unleash the full potential of your team and achieve greater results.

A GUIDED TOUR TO SPEED COACHING

Speed Coaching is both an art and a science. Here is a quick overview of what you will be learning in this book. In the next four pages, you will quickly familiarize yourself with the core ideas presented in different chapters of this book.

Basically, leaders need to understand and master the following to speed-coach their teams.

1. A coaching mindset
2. The focus of coaching
3. A conversational framework
4. Core coaching skills
5. A formula to spot coaching moments
6. Foundation of a Leader-Coachee relationship
7. Knowing their resistance to coach
8. Building a coaching culture

COACHING MINDSET

Without this core belief, no coaching can take place.

1. A Belief in the Coachee's ability to solve their problems
2. A belief that the Coachee has the resources within

Why leaders don't coach more frequently? Because deep down, they believe that the person does not have the capability. And their answers are far superior to theirs. Therefore, they always choose to 'tell' their teams what they should be doing.

COACHING FOCUS

Why do leaders coach their teams? What is the ultimate purpose of coaching?

1. Create self-realization
2. Evoke ownership.

Once leaders believe in their teams' capability and resourcefulness, they choose Coaching more often. They begin to give up their desire to command and control. They refuse to be seen as the most competent person in the room. Leaders recognize that they don't need to be seen as the source of solutions.

To make it happen, they need to embrace the reality that it is challenging to stop giving solutions. What will be the alternative of 'not giving solutions' to them?

There are two:

You create self-realization in them and make them believe in their capability and resourcefulness. Once they become aware that they are more capable and resourceful than they think they are, they start tapping on their untapped strengths.

They start generating ideas they never created before. They develop solutions on their own. They begin finding answers to their problems.

Because they have brought the ideas themselves, they take more ownership of putting them into action. They bounce back more often, and they show reliance. And they start making things happen.

This result is greater engagement and ownership, which is a big miss in the corporate world.

CORE COACHING SKILLS

A coaching mindset supported by necessary coaching skills will transform human potential. There are many skills leader-coaches need to master. Here are two core skills:

1. Deep Listening
2. Power Questioning

To make this engagement and solution focus a reality, leaders need to master two fundamental skills.

First and foremost is listening. When you are not giving solutions and answering their queries, you are left with the only choice – hear.

As a result of more listening, you begin to go in a positive inquiry mode and ask more intelligent questions.

> At this stage, leaders become non-judgmental. They don't attack their teammates. They don't discourage them by dismissing their ideas. They protect their self-image.

A CONVERSATIONAL FRAMEWORK

Leadership is exhibited in daily conversations. All effective conversations follow some structure. Coaching conversations flow when leaders use the following dialogue framework.

1. Direction
2. Analysis
3. Roadmap
4. Empower

Coaching mindset, outcomes, and skills alone can only make a difference if leaders use some framework to structure their coaching conversations. The more leaders practice the framework, the more the talks begin to flow and produce the right results – quicker automatically.

A FORMULA TO SPOT COACHING MOMENTS

Not every interaction is an opportunity to coach. The formula below helps leaders pick up the right moment for coaching.

1. Area
2. Timing
3. Mood

Leaders also learn that not every conversation can be converted into a coaching conversation. They master the art of differentiating when to coach and when to use other management tools. Eventually, leaders recognize that they should only use the coaching style of leadership when the area, timing, and mood are right.

FOUNDATION OF A COACHING RELATIONSHIP

Like all relationships, leaders must lay the foundation of their leader-Coachee relationship based on the following principles.

1. Trust
2. Respect
3. Rapport

Leadership is a relationship. To make it work, leaders need to go to the basics. They find out that having a relationship with their direct reports based on fear, insecurity, hatred, disregard, revenge, and doubt is counterproductive. They must build a relationship where they experience mutual trust, respect, and connection.

KNOW YOUR RESISTANCE TO COACH:

Why do leaders resist the coaching style of leadership? If they know the excuses in advance, they will be better able to overpower them. You will explore in chapter #10, the top three reasons for leaders to resist coaching and how to overcome them?

1. Resistance
2. Importance
3. Preference

BUILDING A COACHING CULTURE:

Helping leaders build a coaching culture is my ultimate objective in writing this book. You will learn to take the following steps to make this transition happen.

1. Identifying the leadership behaviors
2. Clarify your end game
3. Align coaching with your leadership framework
4. Creating a feedback loop
5. Build a powerful coaching team

Coaching culture becomes a reality when leaders at the top level exhibit courage, engage in open dialog, show comfort in giving and receiving feedback, hold each other accountable, and demonstrate total commitment to their ongoing learning and development.

Coaching is an art, and it's far easier said than done. It takes courage to ask a question rather than offer up advice, provide an answer or unleash a solution. Allowing another person to find their way, make their own mistakes and create their wisdom is both brave and vulnerable. It can also mean unlearning our "fix it" habits.'

Brené Brown, author of Rising Strong and Daring Greatly

PART 01

SPEED COACHING CONCEPTS

Coaching is a hugely misunderstood phenomenon. What most of the leaders I interact with know and believe about coaching is usually incorrect. Therefore, this part of the book focuses on helping leaders understand what coaching is and what it is not. It will allow leaders to clarify their misconceptions about coaching and solidify their coaching concepts.

Chapter 01

 **Why Speed Coaching?**

Why Speed Coaching?

In the last twenty years, I have had the privilege to run Executive Coaching and leadership development interventions with over 450 unique organizations in more than 40 countries.

As a Leadership Coach, it was my most exceptional opportunity to actively work with leaders in various industries and geographies. Being a researcher of human behavior, I developed an extraordinary curiosity for determining what makes leaders great. What makes them worthwhile? What makes them deliver superior results consistently?

While working with hundreds of senior business executives, I discovered that some were plain bosses. The difficult ones. Actually, the bad ones. Almost impossible to work with. Hard to get along. People working under them were in a state of agony.

It reminds me of a Swedish study I quoted first in 2015 while training the top leaders of a global bank:

> *'If you work with a bad boss, your chances of getting a heart attack increase to 20%.* **(Swedish Study)**

And here is the bonus. *'If you work with the same bad boss for four years, your risk for a cardiac arrest will mount to a lofty 38%'.*

People in leadership positions (when they fail to provide leadership) can cause heart attacks. Sad. Extremely painful, indeed.

People don't join organizations to inflict heart attacks on them. As an Organizational Psychologist, I firmly believe people show up daily to live their best potential, grow, and make a difference. Whether or not they can turn this intent into action depends on the person they work for.

Not every person people report to at work is a leader. Indeed leadership is a scarce commodity. Most of the people I have encountered in my two decades of research were not leaders. They were bosses. Painful bosses. They were causing people to experience havoc in the workplace. They 'manage' people in a way that their reason to come to work every day disintegrates. People fail to motivate themselves to go to workplaces because of their presence.

> I have also seen that most so-called leaders are best described as *'technicians.* They are great at technical stuff, and no one knows more than they do in their respective fields. They are the masters of the technical craft. However, they know almost nothing about people's mastery, and their knowledge of human psychology is close to zero. They are so full of themselves that they dare learn nothing about improving their people's side.

Some bosses go the 'extra mile' to ruin the lives of those who report to them. They act like bullies, use position power to intimidate people, and become a pain in the neck.

If you are a performance coach or a consultant and have worked with some clients, you do not need to be a NASA scientist to discover that organizations are more or less the same. Their challenges are almost the same. Most organizations have access to the same knowledge, resources, and technology. These companies have the opportunity to hire from the same talent pool.

Then what differentiates a top-performing organization from a low performing one? It took me some 20 years to dig out the answer. And I finally found it out. It's *'leadership.'*

Leadership makes the difference. Organizations win or lose because of their leaders. Leaders have the magic power to build something out of nothing. Leaders, on the other hand, also have this incredible ability to turn triumph into traumas.

I have seen leaders dramatically turning around organizations. They can instill energy, passion, and commitment. I have witnessed leaders expand their performance capacity, break the glass ceiling, and achieve seemingly impossible growth for their organizations.

On the contrary, lousy leadership fails to take advantage of people, their energy, and their capacities. They devastate team spirit. Simply kill the enthusiasm. I have seen organizations becoming hostage to the ego of a few bosses, whose self-centeredness and hunger for personal power led them to destroy management systems and processes. *'I am the system,'* they proclaim. They don't let the system flourish because that threatens their *'self-importance.'*

Repeatedly, research has proven that leadership is a crucial determining factor in organizational performance. A leader's leadership style can influence a company's performance by up to 70%, and that is a significant impact.

Research proves that of all the leadership styles available to leaders today, the coaching style of leadership is the most effective way of interacting with people. Sadly, it is also the least used style of leadership.

The coaching leadership style emphasizes that a leader's job is to empower and enable others. It means that instead of leaders running around all the time, trying to catch up with multiple responsibilities, they should focus on critical priorities and let people solve their day-to-day operational problems themselves.

> Our decade-long research has shown that coaching has emerged as 'the solution' to the problems related to employee engagement. Coaching leaders don't see people as they are; they see them the way they can be. They see people in terms of their strengths, not weaknesses.

In several organizations adopting coaching leadership, we have observed that the moment leaders radiate trust in the capability of their direct reports, it instills confidence, engagement, and commitment in their teams.

Authentic leaders are comfortable in their skin. They don't feel threatened by the talented people around them. They don't get insecure when others bring better ideas to the table. Instead, they take advantage of their teammates' creativity, potential, and knowledge.

THE WHY BEHIND SPEED COACHING

What is the primary job of a leader?

I have been asking this question to hundreds of CEOs and business leaders. One of the most frequent response is *'to deliver results.'*

They all are correct. However, leaders remain so overwhelmed by producing results that they mostly forget the other side of their role's coin. And what is that?

'Developing people.' Yes, developing people and helping them advance in their careers, facilitating them to see the best in them, and guiding them to realize their full potential.

Leaders carry two primary responsibilities on their shoulders. Results and people, and their job is to produce results and develop people—both at the same time.

Leaders are good at getting results through people. Yet, they fail to grow their potential. This responsibility of maximizing their potential is usually outsourced to the HR teams. People go for a two-day 'development' training, and then for the rest of the year, it's only about results. No development.

'You cannot outsource this key responsibility of yours.' I argue with the leaders.

'But we don't have time to train, coach, and mentor our people.' This is how they counter-argue.

To shift their mindset, in my 'Speed Coaching' training for leaders, I take them through this exercise:

'WHAT DO YOU EXPECT FROM YOUR TEAM'?

I present them with a sheet that has this question at the top. Their list goes non-stop. The key themes that always top the list are:

- Be reliable
- Deliver assignments on time

- Follow my instructions
- Keep promises
- Manage their time better
- Challenge themselves
- Take the initiative
- Show a greater sense of responsibility
- Take ownership of their job
- Think out of the box
- Keep me posted on progress without me always chasing them

'WHAT DO YOU THINK YOUR TEAM EXPECTS FROM YOU'?

I give them another piece of paper with this question on the top. *'What do you think your team expects from you'?*

Their immediate reaction is silence. Complete silence. Many of them never thought this way before. Then they begin to reflect. Putting themselves in the shoes of their direct reports. Some of them for the first time. The typical list is like this:

- more clarity
- Sense of direction
- Support
- Information sharing
- Encouragement
- Motivation
- Being with them in stressful situations
- Give them feedback
- Recognize their role
- Appreciate an excellent performance
- Help them advance in their careers
- Coach them
- Trust them
- Tell them that they matter

- Show them their career path
- Grow their potential

This realization creates a different atmosphere in the room. I challenge the audience to pick up the top themes in both questions. And the answer is always the same:

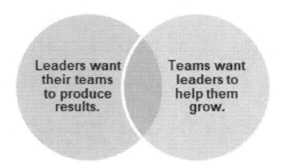

Leaders don't have time to pay attention to the growing needs of their people. And consequently, people fail to produce the desired results.

Leaders become frustrated. They feel pressure from the top. In business, the result is everything. They push the growth agenda aside. Pass on the burden to their teams, expecting them to deliver results.

People in a state of fear go frozen. They hesitate to make any decision on their own. For every tiny thing, they approach the leader for the answers. It burdens leaders with too much dependability on them. This overdependence of their teams on them overwhelms them. They feel overburdened with work, leaving little time for them to work on more strategic goals.

WHAT IS THE CURE?

Research has proven that *speed coaching* is the best way forward.

I have observed in different cultures and countries in my extensive travel for leadership interventions that almost all leaders these days understand significance of coaching. They believe in coaching, and they agree on the benefits coaching offers. Many of them have been provided world-class training in coaching by their organizations. Some also received coaching certifications. I have seen those beautifully framed certificates on their office walls.

Yet, when I ask them, *'how frequently do you coach your people?'* They go silent.

When was the last time you coached one of your team members?

'Cannot recall' is generally the answer of over 85% of leaders.
'What stops you from coaching your people more often?' I ask leaders around the world.
'Lack of time' always tops the list.
I have been swamped.
I don't get the time.
I am pressed with other more critical assignments.
I don't know where my time goes.
I needed to find a solution for them.

I have been training Executives on making a career transition. Many of them successfully transitioned from being executives to becoming Executive Coaches. I have actively facilitated their certification programs and passed out almost 250 executive coaches through my Coach-Training interventions. It was a rigorous process, and it usually took them 6-9 months to complete the coursework and earn the certification.

However, I had this understanding that teaching coaching skills to leaders would follow different path. I re-vamped my processes, coaching frameworks, methodologies, and schedules to best suit busy executives' lives.

'My main job is to produce results. If I sit in the office and coach my direct reports, who will ensure results?

They needed a solution beyond just a 'quick fix,' addressing the growing need of their teams, and at the same time, doesn't require an extra time commitment. Time is something that every executive is challenged by, and almost nobody has time to run one-hour-long coaching sessions with their teams. There standard response is something like this:

They were entirely correct. Their argument was persuasive. It was a fact that they didn't have hours, and then they didn't even have minutes. It was hard for them to commit time to coach. This was the time to give birth to a new coaching concept. This was the time for *speed coaching*.

I designed a two-day, extensive, hands-on program for leaders. I tried it with the C-level leaders of top organizations. They all loved it. *'We never thought coaching would be this fun,'* was the response of most of them. The concept's beauty was that they didn't have to 'block' additional time in their calendar to coach. After all, they were not supposed to be a formal coach with their team.

I firmly believe that developing a formal coaching relationship with Line Managers is counterproductive to the coaching process. It never works. Line managers should never assume an official coaching role with their teams. Employees hardly open up to their bosses.

Employees would never dare to share their true feelings, obstacles, and troubles if they already have a trust deficit. After all, who will dare say to the boss that they are the primary source of pain in their lives?

Leaders needed a tool that was spontaneous, informal, and non-threatening. And it shouldn't add an extra load to their work. Speed coaching seemed to have an answer to their distress. In two days, we taught them all the basic coaching concepts.

They learned to develop a coaching mindset. They learned how to use the DARE coaching framework, endorsed by World's #1 Leadership Coach, Sir Marshall Goldsmith. They learnt how to structure their conversations. They practiced all the necessary tools and skills to coach their teams.

They were excited about returning to the workplace and putting all they had learned into practice. During the training, they had mastered the necessary art of turning any ordinary interaction into a robust coaching conversation. And the best news was that they didn't have to text or email to their direct reports, *'tomorrow at 11:30 am, I will coach you.'*

They were not supposed to tell their direct reports in advance or make them realize during the conversational process that they were being coached. In fact, in speed coaching, if your direct reports spot you coaching them, it is considered a foul.

The key is not to get caught by any radar. The whole aim of speed coaching is to develop your team by raising their self-awareness about the challenges and igniting their sense of responsibility to act on their own solutions.

In a companywide internal review at Google in 2013 to establish what made an effective manager, *"being a good coach"* came top of a long list—trumping technical expertise. The millennial generation, who already constitute the workforce's largest segment, demands coaching from their managers.

ICF's Global CEO and Executive Director Magdalena stated, "Millennials are expected to make up half the global workforce by 2020, and many aspire to leadership roles. Millennials will make a huge impact on shaping the culture. Organizations must know how to help them grow and prepare for the challenges and opportunities of the future".

International Coach Federation conducted a worldwide study surveying 670 leaders, including human resources, learning and development, talent management professionals; managers and leaders; individual contributors; and internal coach practitioners. The study also incorporated in-depth interviews with four subject matter experts from the HR and talent development fields.

ICF's study has revealed that developmental opportunities and flexible work arrangements are the most appealing benefits and workplace characteristics. Most respondents demonstrated an understanding that managers and leaders who use coaching skills are more effective in their roles. When asked to describe the most effective management style, here are the two top methods that 670 respondents across the globe wanted their line managers to use while leading them:

1. The collaborative style of leadership
2. The coaching style of leadership

Furthermore, this research pointed to the business case for building a powerful coaching culture. Respondents with strong coaching cultures reported that 61 percent of their employees are highly engaged, compared to 53 percent from organizations without strong coaching cultures.

> Forty-six percent of respondents in organizations with strong coaching cultures reported above-average revenue growth to industry peers versus 39 percent of all other organizations.

Like many buzzwords in business, most people thought coaching would soon vanish. Coaching has passed the test of time. Coaching is way beyond 'flare of the month.' It's a serious leadership development tool.

Once you begin to use the coaching style of leadership, you won't allow any other style to catch your attention. Most leaders I trained in coaching leadership style have adopted coaching as a new way of living. After all, all leaders want commitment from their teams, not just the compliance.

What does your team give you consistently? Commitment or compliance?

Chapter 02

Speed Coaching
Fundamentals for Leaders

Speed Coaching
Fundamentals for Leaders

A farmer sitting in his yard saw an unknown horse entering his gate. He asked everyone whose horse was that, but no one claimed. The horse didn't have any identity mark. His friends suggested he keep the horse. However, he was determined to return it to the owner.

'Why would you make that futile effort? No one knows where the horse belongs to?' Everyone around him was discouraging.
He remained committed.

He rode the horse. And let him choose where to go. The horse moved in one direction, and he kept quiet. At regular intervals, the horse kept side-tracking, sometimes for the grass or upon seeing his fellow horses.

And when it went too long, the rider gently redirected the horse, bringing it back on track. The horse walked into a village; the rider had never been several miles away from his own.
The horse stopped in front of a house. A man came out and was overjoyed to have his prized horse back home.

'Thank you, gentleman. But how did you know it was my horse and belonged here? The man asked the farmer with a sign of amazement on his face.

The farmer smiled and said, *'I had no idea it was your horse, and I didn't know he belonged here. But I believe the horse did. All I did was keep him on the track.'*

This one-story captures every concept I will reveal in this book. I always use this story to help people understand what coaching is.

Coaching is not telling people what to do. Coaching is not commanding, and coaching is not ordering. Coaching is not teaching. Coaching is not giving instructions.

COACHING IS ABOUT HELPING SOMEONE GAIN THEIR OWN INSIGHTS IN A SITUATION.

Coaching believes in the capability and wisdom of the person before you. Instead of teaching, a coaching leader helps others access their untapped knowledge, understanding, and experiences. Coaching encourages people to develop their insights.

With the traditional management style, you answer questions. People present their quarries to you and expect you to solve their problems. Coaching is the opposite. As a coaching leader, you ask questions; they give the answers.

Do you know why? Because they know the answers.

Like a lost horse, people know exactly where they have to reach, who they are, and what their destination is. However, they sometimes get lost, and they get side-tracked. Your role as a coaching leader is to believe in them. Gently and politely bring them back on track. Your job is not to dictate but to tell them where they belong.

'As an accountability partner, leader empowers the team
to choose and follow their success path responsibly;
to unleash their full potential.' - *Qaiser Abbas.*

The person being coached gains increased clarity regarding the situation or topic, enabling them to progress. A coach facilitates discussion that increases an individual's awareness, insight, and available choice in a situation.

The leader-coach uses the advanced skill of listening, questions, and reflection to create a powerful Coachee experience.

Remember, coaching is not telling people what you think they should do. Coaching is about helping someone gain insights into a situation.

UNDERSTANDING COACHING

In my *'Speed Coaching'* Training programs, I ask people to pick up a partner in the audience. One of them becomes the boss and the other direct report. I then ask bosses to say the following to their reports:

- Look, I am the expert here
- I know the answers
- I will tell you what to do
- Follow my instructions

I then ask bosses how they felt saying this. Their ego goes high—they feel self-importance. I also ask reports to share their feelings.

I have run this exercise multiple times. Direct reports always feel bad. After all, no one likes to be treated like this.

Then I ask them to go back to their partner, saying the following to them:

- You are the expert
- You know better
- What do you think?
- You decide

> Coaching is not telling people what you think they should do.
> Coaching is helping people be the very best they can be

This time, I asked the direct reports about their feeling. They report being valued and connected. Surprisingly, bosses also feel good in the second phase of the exercise. They, too, feel connected.

The second phase of the exercise represents the coaching leadership style.

DIFFERENCE BETWEEN COACHING AND MENTORING

Mentoring and coaching are two different worlds. And yet, people keep using these terms interchangeably.

According to HBR, most managers don't know how to coach, and most confuse coaching with consulting or mentoring. Fortunately, the research shows managers can learn how to coach and improve their coaching skills in just 15 hours, which is why our 2-day experiential workshops are ideal.

To me, there are four significant distinctions between coaching and mentoring:

Distinction #1: **Relationship**

The first one is the relationship. I have had the privilege of being mentored by the legendary Tony Buzan. I always saw him on a higher pedestal. The association was never equal. In our meetings, Tony would speak 95% of the time. My job was to listen. Take notes.

Whereas things are different with Marshall Goldsmith, Coachee has to speak most of the time in his presence. He will make you feel equal. None of you is on a higher pedestal, and it's a relationship between two similar adults. Every insight is heard. He will ask powerful questions and help you build your ideas.

Distinction #2: **Expertise**

The second distinction is expertise. I threw away what I already knew during my full-day interaction with Brian Tracy. All I wanted was to pay attention to his expert views. Because he is the expert. A mentor is generally someone who is a guru in their field. A mentor is a *'done it, been there'* type of person.

On the contrary, Will Linssen, one of the greatest coaches of all time, will make you feel like the expert because you are. The coach is only the subject matter specialist. How could he know more than you about your expertise? The coach is the only expert in the coaching process. This is the hardest thing for the leaders and coaches to digest in my training programs. They like to believe that no one knows more than they do.

Distinction #3: **Solution**

The third distinction is the solution. In a mentoring relationship, the mentor is responsible for creating the solution. Based on their knowledge, expertise, and experience, mentors produce solutions.

However, in coaching, the best solution is with the Coachee. As coaches, our job is to stimulate the thought process and provide the Coachee with a safe environment to express their ideas.

Distinction #4: **Tools**
The fourth distinction is around tools. A mentor's primary mechanism is advising, whereas a coach's vital tool is 'questioning.'

When you operate as a command and control leader, you see yourself one up in the relationship as 'the' expert, who is responsible for creating solutions to all problems in your domain and advising your team all the time.

However, when you choose to be a coaching leader, you operate from a position of equality, believing in the expertise of the person reporting to you, without any pressure to come up with solutions. You rely on intelligent questioning to help the person grow.

As a coaching leader, you fully understand that you have not reached the desired leadership level if you are the most intelligent person in your department.

If your team does not know more than you and doesn't have more capability, it's a sign of an insecure leader. Learning to coach enables individuals and groups to perform more effectively and enjoyably, and you help them unlock their potential and sustain high performance in your organization.

DIMENSION	COACH	MENTOR
Relationship	Equal	On a higher pedestal
Expertise	The Coachee is the expert	A mentor is an expert

Solutions	With the Coachee	With the mentor
Tool	Questioning	Advising

HOW TO PRODUCE RESULTS?

As a leader, your performance is judged based on your results. To produce results, you must influence the behaviors and actions of the people working with you. Getting things done through people requires real art.

In his ground-breaking book, 'Coaching for Performance,' Sir John Whitmore states that bosses use various methods to gain compliance. I call them the leadership choices. These choices are available to anyone who wish to achieve results through others. I ran my research to discover these styles. I actively worked with the line managers and the HR leaders to deeply study the leaders' leadership styles. I was asked to teach speed coaching.

We also interacted with the direct reports of my training participants before the training. We gathered in-depth data about the way they were managing their teams. We studied what results they produced and how did they produce them?

Initially, their direct reports were unwilling to share their deepest feelings and experiences. They were fearful of the consequences. Once they were provided with the necessary security, they opened up. And this is what we found out.

Choice #1: **DO AS I SAY**

The leaders' favorite style was to pass out orders. This, indeed, is the most widely used tool to ensure compliance. The top benefit is that the one who gives the order enjoys feeling in control. People are required to execute the orders.

> 'Most of the time, these orders are given to us without asking us for our opinion. Many times, these orders have no relevance to the ground reality. We don't dare to disagree with the boss. The price is too high.' Their direct report reveals.

The downside of giving orders is that it upsets the team. No one likes to be ordered, and this surely demotivates the team. Also, it has been observed that people show compliance when the 'director' is there. However, they behave differently in the absence of the boss. The fact is that resented employees deliver poor performance.

Choice #2: **LET ME TELL YOU THE BENEFITS OF IT**

Sometimes, tired of giving direct orders or feared with resentment from the team, bosses lay out their great idea on the table and attempt to persuade.

This is an indirect way of ordering. Everyone in the team finds out what the boss wants. Nobody dares to go against the boss's will. After all, everyone finds out why the boss is persuading them. They smile inside. Figure out the hidden agenda of the boss and follow the 'untold' instructions.

Leaders mistakenly believe that they have created a democratic culture. However, deep down, they know that team didn't have a choice to oppose their idea. The fact is that nothing has changed much, and people are still just following instructions.

Choice #3: **LET THE BEST IDEA WIN**

Leaders sometimes initiate a debate to give the impression that it's an open forum.

Everybody is encouraged to share their ideas. Bosses try breaking resistance by asking everyone to present their perspective. Diverse viewpoints are presented, and opinions are pooled.

Bosses show a willingness to follow a path other than their own. But deep down, they are fixated on their ideas. If they see the debate going in a direction, they don't approve of; they will jump back to either convincing or ordering mode.

When bosses use this style, everyone feels involved. However, it is a slow process. Another downside is that the team loses faith in the process when the boss reverts to convincing or ordering.

Choice #4: **DO WHATEVER YOU WANT; I AM OUT OF IT**

That's not leadership, and this is pure surrender. When leaders repeatedly see their team not carrying out their instructions, they become frustrated. They fail to see the disconnect between their orders and on-ground issues.

This frustration turns into anger. Bosses don't see it working. They run out of ideas. Their teams don't volunteer to share their ideas deliberately. Out of sheer frustration, bosses choose to escape. They quit responsibility. They leave everything. Giving an impression to the team that they are free to choose whatever they want.

The team may perform poorly because of low awareness of certain aspects of the job. There is no discussion on the way forward. Leaders abruptly quit and have yet to learn what the team will do. They are blind to the consequences.

Surrendering seldom serves the purpose. The team feels obliged or dumped on to take responsibility rather than accepting responsibility. Hence the willingness to take full ownership of the results remains at an all-time low.

Choice #5: **LET'S CO-CREATE A SOLUTION**

This style is called coaching. Through an interactive, thought-provoking, and mind-expanding dialogue, the employees choose to take action.

Now the leader knows what their direct report will do, and the employee has full knowledge and ownership of the results. Both are on the same page. No order, no persuading, no debate, no escape. Simply collaboration. Pure speed coaching.

IT'S TIME TO EMBRACE SPEED COACHING

Gone are the days when you could order people and expect compliance. Leaders are not appreciated when they drop orders from their place  of position. More and more businesses realize that leadership with practical coaching skills is a more desired pathway to progress.

Many studies have revealed that employees no longer want to work to keep their job. They want to work to be a part of something bigger than themselves. They expect their leaders to engage them. Leaders who know how to create belonging and influence can motivate their teams.

> Leaders report that initially, they needed help to embrace speed coaching. It made things slower than faster. It was easy to tell than ask questions and expect employees to come up with their answers. It required patience, which is becoming rare these days.

However, after repeatedly operating from a coaching position, it became their second nature to speed coach. It turned out to be much more rewarding in the longer run. Their teams started solving problems independently, and leaders had more time to focus on futuristic and strategic issues.

Leaders worldwide are using speed coaching to fast-track performance and potential. This is your chance to up your leadership game and take it to a new level.

PART 02

SPEED COACHING SKILLS

This part of the book is about helping coach-leaders build the core competencies required to coach their teams whenever the opportunity arises. Based on the **LEAP Model**, leaders will go through four stages of becoming a coach-like leader. You will **L**earn, **E**xperiment, **A**pply and **P**ractice the coaching mindset, skillset, and framework to get the most from speed-coaching at workplace.

LEARN
The Basics of Speed Coaching

Chapter #3 – **Mindset of a Coach-Like Leader**
- Coachee is Capable
- Coachee is Resourceful

Chapter #4 – **Focus of a Coaching Leader**
- Raise Self-Awareness
- Evoke Ownership

 The Mindset of a Coach-Like Leader

The Mindset of a Coach-Like Leader

A 7-year-old boy came back home from school and handed over a sealed letter to his mother, which was given to him by his teacher.

Mother opened the letter and went quiet. 'What's in the letter'? Asked the boy with relentless curiosity. Mother smiled and said;

> **"Your son is a Genius. This school is not the right place for him, and there are no efficient teachers to train him. So, please train him yourself."**

After many years, the boy became the innovation machine, with more than 1000 inventions. He invented the light bulb, the camera, the phonograph, etc.

I am sure you would have already figured out who this boy was by now. Yes, he was Thomas Edison.

After many years, he was looking for some documents in his mother's cupboard and found a letter. He immediately recognized the envelope that he had handed over to his mother half a century ago.

He was shocked to see what the teacher had written for his mother that day. The letter read:

> **"School cannot allow your son to attend classes anymore; he is mentally impaired. He is rusticated."**

That fact is Thomas A. Edison was a declared mentally deficient child. But his **mother turned him into "The Genius of the century."**

My question is, how did his mother do that?

What is it that Edison's teacher missed seeing in him? How could his mother spot his potential that almost no one did?

What mindset allowed Edison's mother to see a superstar in him while his teacher gave up on him?

The same mindset can help leaders turn ordinary teammates into remarkable performers. In this chapter, I am going to decode the coaching mindset. You will see the complexities of the coaching world turning into the simplicities of daily life.

WHAT DO COACHING LEADERS BELIEVE?

All coaching spurs from two fundamental beliefs:

- Coachee is capable
- Coachee is resourceful

Edison's mother *believed* in her son's ability. She *knew* her son was going to be a superstar.

She didn't think, assume or hypothesize that her son was capable. She *believed* that her son was a genius. Her belief in her son's capability and resourcefulness led her to see, do, and communicate things differently.

Her faith allowed her to invest her time, energy, and resources to grow Edison's potential.

On the contrary, Edison's teacher *believed* he was a lost case, and she accepted that the boy had nothing special in him. It was her *mindset* that prevented her from seeing the capability and resourcefulness in Edison. And this very mindset motivated her to give up on Edison.

Whether you invest in helping people grow or give up on them; depends entirely on your *mindset*.

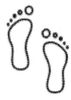

When leaders act from the position of a coach, they start believing in the ability of the individual to create ideas, decide for themselves, and move their situation forward.

Let's explore the coaching mindset in more detail.

MINDSET #1

COACHEE IS CAPABLE

When you wear coaching shoes, you are no longer a boss. You are a coach. And the person you will converse with is no more a subordinate. S/he is your Coachee.

This Coach-Coachee relationship will open doors to new possibilities for you, your team, and your organization.

Let's start with two reflective questions:

1. As a leader, do you believe in the capability of your direct reports?
2. Do you believe that people in your team are more capable than you think they are?

THE MINDSET MIRACLE

In a study, teachers were told that the class they would teach represented the brightest scholarship-holder students. They are the best of the best. 'You are being given the cream of the school.' They were briefed.

At the end of the semester, students surpassed expectations. They over-delivered and outperformed every other school.

The same teachers were given another set of students in a different class. This time they were told that these students have some learning disabilities. And they are mentally challenged.

As expected, the results were dismal at the end of the semester.

Teachers didn't know that in both classes they taught, students were almost the same in academic performance. There were no scholarship holders or mentally challenged students. They were just average students, randomly allocated to two classes without using any scientific method. They were randomly picked up out of a hat.

However, teachers' perceptions about the class they were teaching made all the difference. Teachers' view of students' capability influenced their performance both in a negative and positive sense.

My question is, can a leader's perception of their direct reports' ability impact their performance?

It does.

When leaders believe in their people's capability, strength, and potential, the team does respond to the leader's expectations.

This self-fulfilling prophecy of leaders works magically. When leaders don't believe in their team's capability, it gets communicated whether or not the leader says it.

WHAT IS YOUR LENS?

 Leaders can see their direct reports through the lens of the problem or a lens of possibility.

When leaders use the problem lens, they choose to eliminate the team. However, a possibility lens encourages them to invest tremendous energy in developing them.

What is your lens?

We always respect those who view us through a lens of possibility. We feel a sense of gratitude towards people who see a better person is us. They made us feel more capable than we thought we once were.

We might also recall some people who used their problem lens on us. They didn't believe in our capability. They didn't see any good in us. Their mindset led them to give up on us.

Do you believe others have tried both lenses on you?

What was the impact of others using their lens on you?

Which lens shaped your current reality?

Which lens weakened your self-belief?

Are you still under the influence of a problem lens someone once saw you through?

Isn't it sad that when others viewed us through a problem lens, it diminished our self-confidence? How come their view of us became ours? Why did we borrow their lens to see how capable we are?

At the same time, seeing through a possibility lens allowed us to see ourselves as capable and resourceful. The possibilities that only they could see in us became the reality of our lives. Isn't it magical?

I am sensitizing you so you can see the impact of seeing someone from these two lenses. The effect of choosing your lens can be life-lasting on people around us.

The good news is that the as a coach, you don't have a choice to use one of these lenses. Do you know why? Coaches only carry one lens. They have only one. The possibility lens. They only see people as capable and resourceful. Do you know why? Because they are.

To me, there is no other way of looking at people. They do have the capability. But it is hidden. Your job as a leader is to bring that capability to the surface.

A leader's doubt in someone's capability sows the seed of doubt in the person's mind. They are especially concerned about their stated goals. When leaders believe in their capability, they empower to solve their own problems.

> **'As a coach, if you say one thing but think another, somehow it communicates.'** Julie Starr, Author of 'The Coaching Manual'

WHEN LEADERS DON'T BELIEVE IN THE CAPABILITY OF THEIR TEAM

What is the opposite of belief?

Doubt.

Think of a person in your team that you are not much confident about their capability.

'If you don't believe in one of your direct reports, would you give her an important assignment?' I asked this question in my recent training.

'Seeing the importance of the assignment, I will not consider her.' Most of the people responded.

Only some were willing to give them a try.

'I would rather give it to someone I fully trust their capability.' was the consensus.

Now if we keep bypassing that person for growth assignments, where will the person's career lead to? Don't you think the person is going to experience some demotivation?

Leaders are primarily under severe time pressures. They have no time to develop a new person's skill (and, more importantly, the confidence) to trust with the job.

And even if they try this new person, they somehow radiate their lack of trust in their capability. People don't listen to what you say. They listen to your non-verbal clues, body language, expressions, etc.

What will happen if the leader-coach secretly believes that the Coachee (their team member) is incapable and un-resourceful?

It will damage both you and the person. Let's start with you:

Your performance as a leader-coach will be below average. Since you don't believe in the person's capability, your ability to support the individual will be flawed. You will quickly give up on the person. Investment in the coaching process will go futile.

The person you were coaching will also suffer. She will settle for less instead of pursuing higher goals. The person will stop challenging themselves, and she will learn to cope with their weaknesses. Your lack of belief in them will undermine their confidence making goal achievement less likely.

Moreover, the person will find it difficult to trust someone else when they believe in their capability.

Why do leaders use problem lenses more often?

Because this is the lens that they were seen through mostly, In their own experience, finding faults is easy. When we are on a hunt, we do find some.

The lens we use to view our capabilities can influence our ability to see potential in our team. If I think something is impossible, others won't make it possible.

Here's my advice for limiting leaders.

NEVER PLACE YOUR LIMITS UPON OTHER PEOPLE

EXERCISE: PERSPECTIVES

 I have used this exercise successfully to alter leaders' mindsets. I ask my participants to think of a person they regularly work with. Then, I ask them to use the following perspectives, one at a time and see the person through this lens.

1. I think this person is a problem
2. I think this person has a problem
3. This person is on a learning journey and is capable, resourceful, and full of potential.

I would also like you to run this exercise. Pick up someone on your team. Now spend some time reflecting on the above perspectives. Done?

I would like you to reflect on the below questions and see how a lens change produced a change in the person.

1. What did you see in the person with different mindsets?
2. How did your feelings and emotions change with each mindset?
3. What did you believe about the person's potential in each situation?
4. How did your attitude change with each perspective?
5. What is your preferred mindset daily?

This exercise changes everything. Participants feel surprised. It's mind-blowing to see how your attitude, emotions, and behavior changes toward the person once you make a shift in your lens.

HOW DO YOU BUILD OTHERS' SELF-BELIEF?

 All sincere leaders strive to build the self-confidence of their teams. They make sure that people working with them believe in their own self-worth. How do they do that? I have interviewed hundreds of them and found the following key insights.

The top strategy they use is changing how they think about their people, and this helps them release the desire to control them. One of these leaders' most challenging and decisive actions is crushing their belief in their superior abilities. They stop thinking they are the smartest and their ideas are the best.

To build the belief of their people, coaching leaders assist them so that they are no longer dependent on them to provide them solutions.

COACHEE IS RESOURCEFUL

Have you ever seen a team working in gold mines? Their job is to dig gold.

While digging for gold, they encounter too many unwanted materials like dust, mud, sand, stones, etc. They get everything else but gold, and yet they keep digging.

What makes them dig? Why do they do that?

I still remember the golden worlds of the CEO of a gold-digging company. He said, **'To find one ounce of gold, we must handle thousands of tons of mud. The key is to ignore the mud. And keep your eyes on the gold.'**

People have many flaws. As a master gold digger, you need to develop a unique eye for gold.

Anyone can see weaknesses in you. But a true teacher, mentor, and coach will ignore what they don't need to see in you. They keep digging deeper until they discover what they are looking for—your talent, potential, and strengths.

Everyone has resources. But only some discover them. Only a few can tap into those resources. However, it's difficult to ignore the one who finds the resources in you.

As a leader, you need to believe that people have reservoirs of energy, capability, strengths, and resources. Your job is to go deeper. But don't go deeper alone. Take them with you, and engage them in this journey of exploration.

Everyone has potential. How much is there? How much have they already used? How much is left? Who knows?

Before you take them on this journey of self-exploration, please be warned. You can only take them to a level you have personally experienced yourself.

> **You wouldn't take them any Fur thus than you have gone yourself.**

I want you to stop reading the book and run the below experiment. Find someone around you. It can be your colleagues, partner, friend, spouse, or whomever you find.

Talk to your partner, ask about their top three goals in life, and then answer the following question:

1. How do you feel about the goals this person has described?
2. How achievable do you believe this person's goals are?
3. What do you think about this person's capability compared to their goals?
4. If you were to support their goals, how committed do you feel toward their success with these goals?

COACHEE HAS THE ANSWERS WITHIN

Try this exercise keeping in view your team. One member at a time. How do you feel about them after the exercise? Answering the above four questions will help you understand your coaching mindset.

Did it help you understand how you view people and their potential?

You will surely see your team's untapped reservoir of resources when you start believing in the following.

- People in my team possess more capability than they currently express.
- My team does have the potential to achieve more meaningful goals. There is more in my team waiting to be released.
- I must also look beyond their current performance and focus on their potential.
- I need to stop fitting in the performance boxes.

I have had the honor of learning from the father of coaching, Sir John Whitmore. He says that people have far more potential than what they exhibit.

To get more out of people, we must believe they have more. How much is there? What reserves do they have? We don't know. How to get it out? We need to learn from the fact that people behave very differently in crisis. You might have seen mothers showing the superhuman capacity to save their children in incredibly tough situations.

The potential is always there. Crisis becomes the catalyst. But why are we waiting for the crisis? Why can leaders not be the catalyst? And help people unleash their true potential.

Instead of acting as a catalyst to unleash their potential, leaders become a wall, not letting their people grow their potential.

Imagine you asked one of your direct reports to prepare a report. The person works very hard to complete the information. After seeing the message, you shout at the person and say, *'You are useless.'*

It's a direct assault. Killing. Very harsh. It must be heartbreaking for the person who spent hours preparing the report. Would the person leave motivated?

Look at another possible response. *'This document is crap.'* You say.

Here you didn't attack the person but discarded the work. Still very disrespectful, and you should have told the person what wrong or needed improvement was.

Another response could be this, *'Content is good, but the layout is pathetic.'*

The person is still under fire. You appear to be ruthless, *and pathetic* is too unforgiving. It only tells a little to the person what changes to be made.

Imagine you asked this question. *'How do you feel about working on this report'?*

Or you went a step ahead and said, *'What do you think is the essential purpose of this report? Who do you think is the target audience for this report? What will they appreciate in this report?'*

As a coaching leader, you prefer to ask questions four and five before asking the person to work on the report. This way, you will empower your team to understand the significance of this assignment, see the big picture, build alignment, and know the sensitivities. All in advance. They can spot the pitfalls and suggest a solution to those potential problems.

Engaging the person in this two-way dialogue will help your direct report to achieve the following:

- More awareness of the situation
- More clarity before taking action

You will also notice that simply verbalizing your thoughts and feelings is sometimes enough to gain a new perspective.

A short investment of time in the **right direction** would create **different results.**

Most of the time, leaders don't ask their team for input or comfort them to speak up. Hence, people don't volunteer to suggest their ideas. Therefore leaders fail to take advantage of the reservoir of creativity waiting to be released inside their teams.

ASSESS YOURSELF

Answer the following questions from a neutral standpoint. Without being defensive. Without appearing to be what you are not. Be authentic. 100%. Now have a look at the questions:

- How often do you deprive others of a learning opportunity by taking their work?

- What stops you from allowing others to learn and develop?
- How can you recognize situations where others are needlessly depending on you?

COACHING IS A WAY OF BEING

Coaching is not a method, a technique, or a tool. It's a way of life. It's a way of being. Once you see the rewards of speed coaching, you won't like to adopt any other form of leading or living.

You can only coach people once you firmly believe in yourself and the capability, resourcefulness, and potential of those you lead. This belief lets you focus on strengths, solutions, and future success.

Instead of catching people on the blunders they made, you focus on their achievements. You stop noticing their past mistakes and start seeing their future success. Also, you help them see the good that you see in them.

You stop seeing problems in them, and you begin to see possibilities. Instead of focusing on their weakness, you start seeing their strengths.

ACTION STEPS:

- Always believe in people. Radiate trust in their capability, strengths, and resources.
- Give people a chance to unleash their full potential
- Stop judging them
- Remember, coaching is not about past mistakes; it's about future possibilities.
- Move the Coachee from the current to the preferred future state.
- Don't attack anyone's self-image. Don't label them.

Impactful Coaching Conversations

- Find the coaching moment and help them learn from the experience.
- Coaching is a way of being

Focus on strengths, solutions, and future success, not on past mistakes, problems, and weaknesses.

Chapter 04

 Focus of a Coaching Leader

Focus of a Coaching Leader

"Strength and growth come only through continuous effort and struggle."
— **Napoleon Hill**

It was December 12, 2019. My *'Coaching Powerclass* for Leaders' was about to begin. I had so many opening ideas planned. And yet, just before a few minutes of the class, I decided to use this powerful story. The story is not new, but the perspective is.

There was a little boy who loved caterpillars. One day he found one, took him home and made a house for it. He watched this caterpillar every day, ensuring he had plenty of food & water.

After a few days, the caterpillar started creating a cocoon; he would go through a metamorphosis and become a butterfly. It was an exciting view, and the little boy couldn't wait to see the butterfly!

One day, a small hole appeared in the cocoon, and the butterfly struggled to emerge. The little boy was so excited! But then he noticed the butterfly was working so hard to get out, and it looked like it wouldn't break free!

The little boy was so worried about the butterfly that he decided to help her. He quickly got a pair of scissors and snipped the cocoon to make the hole bigger, and the butterfly emerged!

But the butterfly had a swollen body and tiny shriveled wings. The little boy sat and watched the butterfly, expecting that, at any moment, the wings would dry out, get bigger and expand to support the swollen body.

But it never happened!

The butterfly spent the rest of its life crawling around with a swollen body and shriveled wings.

It never was able to fly. In his kindness and haste, the innocent boy did not understand that restricting the cocoon and the struggle required for the butterfly to get through the tiny opening was God's way of forcing fluid from its body into its wings. It would allow it to be ready for flight once it achieved its freedom from the cocoon.

He then learned that the butterfly was supposed to struggle. The butterfly's struggle to push its way through the tiny opening of the cocoon pushes the fluid out of its body and into its wings. Without the effort, the butterfly would never, ever fly. The boy's good intentions hurt the butterfly irreversibly.

Leaders are not any different. With their best intentions at heart, they deprive people of their wings. They spoon-feed their teams with solutions. Not letting them 'struggle' to find their answers. They forget that this struggle is essential for them to grow their potential, expand their comfort zone, and fly to new heights.

Coach-leaders understand that the best way to encourage and empower their teams is to push them to make an effort and not provide easy answers. They know that struggling is an integral part of any growth experience. Coaching leaders believe that struggle transforms people and allows them to become the best version of themselves.

As a leader, when you see people struggling, ask yourself:

1. Do I believe in their capability and resourcefulness?
2. What can this problem help them learn?
3. How can this experience facilitate their growth?

Impactful Coaching Conversations

**Coaching is helping people transform
from cocoons to butterflies.**

My coaching career's turning point was meeting with Dave Ulrich, the legendary HR Guru, during the 43rd IFTDO conference in Dubai in 2014. I was excited about my maiden chance to share the stage with him.

It was a multi-day conference. I was lucky to have had numerous interactions with him. We were staying in the same hotel.

In one of my conversations with dave, I asked him about the future of leadership. And this is what Dave Ulrich, the world's #1 Management Guru has to say:

'As you progress throughout your career and
transition into leadership roles, one thing becomes
abundantly clear and it's not about you. It's about the
performance of your team and the organization.

 Coaching is an essential aspect of your leadership role. Leaders are reluctant to take time out for coaching. It is sad knowing that while shadowing some top business leaders in their daily work routines, I found them wasting valuable time watching useless funny video clips, aimlessly scrolling through their social feeds, jumping between numerous WhatsApp chats, and sharing that crap in other groups. Yet, sadly leaders didn't have time to coach people.

They need to realize that coaching is not a time wastage activity. It is an investment in people, and it is an investment in the knowledge capital of the organization.

KEY CHALLENGE FOR THE LEADERS

In our leadership study, we have seen leaders struggling with two things.

1. DEPENDENCY:

 Their teams depend too much on them. They have to work even on the weekend to follow up with them and to give them instructions. Sometimes, they have to answer their quarries in the middle of the night.

Many leaders operate in more than one time zones. Their direct reports operate from different countries, and they have to be there to be available to them 24/7. These leaders are too stressed out and internally shattered and burnt out. Their number one worry is to find a way to break this cycle of dependency. So their teams stop depending too much on them.

2. TEAM GROWTH:

 Due to the constant focus on human capital development, organizations are constantly holding leaders accountable for the growth and development of their teams. Sometimes, leaders share their frustrations with me in private conversations. 'I don't know when my team will focus on real work. It's been too much learning, and I wonder when they can use learning to deliver results.' They protest. Helping people grow is their second worry.

This chapter is for you if you have ever been worried about dependency and growth issues.

To address this worry, I decided to dig deeper to know what could be the ultimate purpose of coaching. What is the result that all of us are looking for? What do we want to inculcate in our people?

And whatever it is, we must focus all our energies on that endgame.

I have asked more than half a million leaders this question in recent years. And the answer has always revolved around two key expectations.

1. Leaders want their teams to develop self-realization around their key responsibilities, and they should not be sensitizing their teams on the consequences of not taking timely action. Leaders expect their teams to be self-aware of what is happening inside and outside them.
2. Leaders desire their people to take full ownership of the area of their responsibility. Leaders want their people to act like owners. Take the pain. Follow through till the end. Go the extra mile. Make more effort. All of this is only possible if they own the job.

So let me reveal to you my secret recipe for engaging and motivating people:

1. Raise self-awareness
2. Evoke ownership

The ultimate goal for you as a coach-leader is to achieve the above. Once people inculcate self-awareness (self-realization) and take ownership of their roles and actions, you will break the dependency cycle, and your team will grow exponentially.

RAISE SELF-AWARENESS

I recently coached one executive planning to move to another country with his wife and kids.

He was supposed to resign from his current job and plan to establish a business in Australia or find a suitable job there. His challenge was to motivate himself to design a game plan.

According to him, it was the time constraint that stopped him. He was swamped and overwhelmed with work. His deadline was August 1, and it was mid-April already. And he could not even motivate himself to think and plan.

He wanted me to give him a solution to his problem.

'Imagine this is August's first week. You have just landed at Sydney airport. Because you have been very busy and never got the required motivation to plan a smooth transition, you did nothing. You are standing outside the airport with your family and have no place, money, or work. What will you do? I asked him.

The man was speechless, and I could see his facial expressions changing from shock to frustration to guilt.

'No, no, no, I cannot afford to do that. If I didn't prepare, I wouldn't be able to even take off from here and land in Sydney,' He had much sense of urgency and stress in his tone.

'So how will you find the time and motivate yourself to do the planning'? I asked him.

'I am operating from home today due to this Covid-19 thing. Developing the plan will take a few hours, and I will do that today. And send you the email by the afternoon'. You jolted me, and not doing it is not a choice. Thank you for the wake-up call.'

At 2:23 pm the same day, the email was in my mailbox.
I didn't motivate him. I didn't tell him what to do. I just asked him a question. A power question. The question allowed him to build self-awareness, a realization, an insight. He got a chance to think for himself and see the results of his actions with his own eyes. The question helped him grab two things.

1.   Develop self-awareness about his behavior and the potential cost of it
2.   Take ownership of those consequences

He sent me the email because he could reflect on the two points I mentioned above.
Have you ever told a friend to quit smoking, stating all the dangers and health consequences, but s/he didn't? And one day, s/he tells you that s/he did it without anyone telling, persuading, or threatening them to quit.

'How did you do that'? You ask him
'I saw my 5-year-old son mimicking me holding a cigarette in his hand. I told myself, 'enough is enough.' S/he tells you.
And since then, s/he has never touched a cigarette.

Warnings and lectures didn't make a difference. Self-awareness of the consequences did.

Have you ever seen this FedEx logo before?

Did you ever notice there is an arrow within this logo?

If you have not noticed it before, this will be a good experience. It will be fantastic to move from a time when you are searching and getting frustrated on why everyone can see the arrow and I cannot; to a point where you, too, spot it.

Being able to see the arrow finally would be an Aha experience. This is called a moment of insight. A moment of realization. A moment of finding the truth. Knowing something you didn't know before, acknowledging the presence of something in your life that you never owned before.

WHAT IS SELF-AWARENESS?

When leaders choose to coach during the conversations, the Coachee frequently goes deeper into a state of self-awareness. How do you know as a leader when your Coachee is experiencing this moment of self-realization? Here are some signals:

- The Coachee shares an Aha moment. A moment of complete wow.
- Coachee develops a new insight.
- The Coachee notices something they never saw before
- The Coachee can develop a new perspective
- Coachee starts looking at things in a brand-new manner

- Coachee shares a feeling of knowing things from within
- Coachee embraces a different reality from what they believed in the past.

WHAT DOES THIS SELF-AWARENESS DO?

- Coachee builds greater awareness about self, others, and situations.
- Coachee becomes more attentive to things previously ignored
- Coachee shows more mindfulness
- Coachee becomes alert to events
- Coachee stops looking at the surface and becomes more focused on an in-depth analysis of the situation.
- Coachee experiences more frequently a state of wakefulness.

WHAT IS THE OPPOSITE OF SELF-AWARENESS?

Building greater self-awareness is at the heart of the coaching process. Take the self-awareness out, and there is no coaching. The absence of self-awareness means you will always be at the mercy of others telling you and making you realize the things, events, decisions, and choices impacting your life.

What is the opposite of self-awareness?

- Ignorance of essential elements of your life that can damage you
- Defensiveness in the face of feedback. I need to get the learning.
- Sleepwalking through life avoids confronting important issues that negatively impact the quality of your life.
- Escaping responsibility instead of accepting it.
- Closed-mindedness, not opening up to new ideas and possibilities.
- Excuse-mentality and justifying counterproductive behaviors.

Your best moment as a leader-coach would be when the Coachee, who was initially unable to see the obvious, says something like this:

- "I never thought of it this way."
- "I can't believe I never saw that before,"

And you will know that the Coachee has begun to view things differently. And you know this new knowledge will encourage them to take further action.

This moment of self-realization brings with it an unexplainable delight. From not knowing to knowing is an incredible journey. Let me share a powerful story to help you understand this self-awareness phenomenon.

A sick, pregnant, and utterly hungry Tigress goes hunting one day and finds a herd of goats. She goes after the goats and attacks them desperately. She runs harder without success. The Tigress gets so tired that she collapses in exhaustion giving birth to her cub, and dies.

When the goats return to the field, they find the motherless newborn. Those goats decide to adopt him. The cub grows up mimicking the behaviors of other goats around him. He bleats, and he eats grass. *He believes himself to be a goat.*

Then one day, a big male tiger comes into the goat herd, and all the goats scatter except this little tiger. He is about a year old and looking at this big male tiger, and somehow, he is sensing an affinity with this tiger.

The giant tiger comes over to him and says, *'What's wrong with you?'*

The little one says, *'What do you mean what's wrong with me?'* The giant tiger says, *'What are you doing here? You are acting weird. You are acting like a goat.'*
The little tiger says, *'I am a goat!'*

The big one says, *'No, you're not. You are not a goat.'*
He leads the little tiger over to a pond.

A still pond. He said, *'Now look at yourself.'* The little cub looks at himself, looks at the giant tiger and is confused.
The tiger says, *'come with me.'* He takes him back to his den, and in the shelter, there is some leftover meat from a gazelle that had been his recent kill.

He says to the little tiger, *'Eat this.'*
The little cub says, *'Well, no way. I am a vegetarian.'*
The tiger says, *'Try it. Just feel the taste of it.'*

The little tiger reaches over and takes a bite off the bone.
When that little tiger who thought he was a goat reaches down and tastes some of the meat, he first chokes on the heart. He gags, and then a piece of that meat enters his bloodstream, and the cub begins to stretch.

He bares his claws, opens his mouth wide, and lets out a small roar for the first time.

That first roar isn't very fearsome, and it still needs to be all the roar the tiger will give. I call this first roar the *roar of awakening*. It's the first moment this little cub recognizes that he isn't whom he thought he was.

As a coach-leader, your exceptional achievement would be to help people develop this self-realization that was not what they thought themselves to be. Coaching is magical, and when leaders use this magic tool, people tear out their history and embrace this new realization of who they are.

A lion was always a lion. However, the cub never believed in this truth and kept the identity of a goat. For all those years when he believed he was a goat, he actually was a lion. Likewise, people continue believing in their weaknesses, mistakes, and ineptness for years.

For all those years, they were resourceful, capable, and powerful. And this realization came when someone helped them become more conscious and self-aware.

Telling people what to do shuts the doors of self-awareness for them.

This moment of self-realization is the beginning of a new life. This self-realization comes from awareness which is the product of focused attention, concentration, and clarity.

Aware means *'conscious, not ignorant, knowing'*. Awareness implies knowing something through alertness in observing or interpreting what one sees, hears, feels, etc. Concise Oxford Dictionary:

Coaching leaders help their teams build self-awareness, a high-quality self-generated, relevant input. Self-awareness empowers you to know what is happening around you and understand how it impacts you. Telling people what to do shuts the doors of self-realization for them.

EVOKE OWNERSHIP

Would you like to know leaders' number one expectations from their teams?

Ownership. Yes, you are right. It is ownership.

Leaders wish to have a button installed in their people, making them fully own their jobs and results. The reality is that leaders are chasing their people all the time. 'Why cannot they think like an owner'? The team's unwillingness to own the results is their most intense pain.

Why does coaching produce results? It does because it instills self-awareness, allowing people to take more ownership.

Advice-giving is the opposite. You must be very clear about the complete transaction when advising someone.

Before advising, you had advice in your hand. The other person also had something in their hands, and I call it 'ownership.'

You bring advice to the table, and they bring ownership. When the transaction occurs, you exchange whatever you got on the table. In this trade-off, you leave the table with the ownership (to get things done) and your direct report with the advice (your idea, how to do it).

Advice without ownership of making it happen is of no use.
That's why the advice doesn't work. You might have advised many people who did the opposite. Why? Because your suggestion didn't make sense to them.

People only take ownership of executing ideas and solutions when they think it makes sense. Our thoughts, answers, and advice are very dear to us, and that's why we end up doing what we thought was best for us.

NEVER TRADE ADVICE FOR OWNERSHIP.

The best gift coaching offers is that the advice and ownership remain in the same person's hands. It ensures that no trade-off is taking place.

Nothing exchanges, no transactions between leaders and direct reports.

Coaching leaders engage their teams in meaningful conversations. When such discussions occur, the Coachees experience different insights they would have never shared due to fear of bosses. It dawns on a new way of thinking and behaving in front of them.

The insights build self-awareness and realization to see things from a different perspective.

Responsibility is **crucial for high performance**. When we truly **accept, choose, or take** responsibility for our thoughts and actions, our **commitment** and performance rise.

A SAMPLE **SPEED COACHING** CONVERSATION

See the below-coaching conversation. I would like you to pay attention to how the coach created self-realization in the Coachee that triggered a sense of ownership.

COACHEE: Hi, have you got a couple of minutes?

COACH: Yeah, I have two minutes before the meeting.

COACHEE: I have an issue with a client at the moment and would like to have some advice.

COACH: You might need to think through your feet for yourself. What is going on at the moment?

COACHEE: I am about to slip into the deadline, and this particular client I find intimidating and quite challenging, and I am trying to figure out how to deal with him.

COACH: Okay, it's always challenging, especially when deadlines slip. Okay, so what exactly do you need to take from this conversation?

COACHEE: I need clarity on how to deal with this person and what I will do.

COACH: Okay, so you need to work out what you will do and how you will deal with the situation. Okay, so what have you thought of already?

COACHEE: Well, I feel a bit blank, to be honest, but I know this person likes solutions and doesn't like you to come to them with problems, and I know that he doesn't want me to be explaining why I slipped. He probably wants me to be talking about what's going well, what's working, and the solutions that there were, and also the preps and benefits of these extra three days are going to be.

COACH: I sensed that you have thought about it a lot.

COACHEE: Well, yes, in the face of talking to him, I get nervous, go black, and I don't know what I am going to do, and I don't know.

COACH: Since you know what you must do, it's just the nerves getting in your way, so what's your advice to yourself about this?

COACHEE: My advice to myself is to call him because I know at some point, he is going to be calling me, at some point today, because he is going to be aware because of a couple of the emails I have gone through. If I had preempted that call and taken control, I would be in a better position with him.

COACH: Sounds like a good idea, getting there first.

COACHEE: I think so because otherwise, I am on the back foot with him. I always feel on the back foot with him.

COACH: To get on the front foot, what do you need to do here?

COACHEE: I need to call him. First, I also need to structure what I will say to him. I also think about what he might say and have some answers. Because I know he is quick, I have dealt with him a few times.

COACH: So, it sounds to me like, to get on the front foot, give him a call can work on what he might say and also have to think a little about what he might get back with so that you are prepared for that as well.

Okay, sounds like a plan to me. I do have to jump into this meeting now. How do you feel about doing this?

COACHEE: That's great. I feel much better. Can I call you later to let you know how it went?

COACH: I am sure it will go fantastically well. If you have any other problem, knock on the door if you need to; I am there for you. Good Luck!

COACHEE: Thank You.

In his book Sporting Excellence, David Hemery researched 63 of the world's top performers from over 20 sports. Despite considerable variations in other areas, awareness and responsibility were the two most critical attitudinal factors common to all.

ACTION STEPS

1. Always believe in people. Radiate trust in their capability, strengths, and resources.
2. Develop a mindset that being helpful starts by not taking on others' problems.
3. Focus on developing their leadership skillset.

4. Encouraging own processing, analysis, problem-solving, decision-making, and strategizing.
5. Move the Coachee from the current to the preferred future state.
6. One of the essential points in learning coaching is a focus on receiving feedback and reflection.

Stage 02

EXPERIMENT
With Speed Coaching Skills

Chapter #5 – Speed Coaching Formula
- Area
- Timing
- Mood

Chapter #6 – Core Coaching Skills to Speed Coach
- Deep Listening
- Power Questioning

Chapter 05

 Speed Coaching Formula

Speed Coaching Formula

Leaders and managers cannot and should not act as formal coaches to their teams. Many organizations that I know made this mistake. They trained their executives to become official coaches. They would schedule regular sessions with their teams.

Teams couldn't open up with them. Team members never shared with them how did they exactly feel. Had they been given a chance to have formal coaching with a neutral person, they would have loved to open up and share their deepest worries, concerns, challenges, and vulnerabilities.

Therefore, in my Speed Coaching training, l teach leaders how to master informal coaching. The Coachee engaged in a coaching dialogue without them knowing they were being coached. A master leader-coach utilizes the same principals, methods, frameworks, and tools that a professional executive coach uses. The only difference is that they do it subtly, unannounced.

WHAT IS FORMAL COACHING?

A formalized contracted relationship between a professional coach and a client is identified by clearly defined roles, timelines, goals, and customer expectations.

Informal coaching is different. There is one of the most straightforward definitions of informal coaching by Rob Kramer:

An informal communication process between two people can be utilized in almost any context where the Coachee has a situation in which more than one solution is possible.

THE ROLE OF LEADER, MANAGER, AND COACH ARE MUTUALLY EXCLUSIVE OF ONE ANOTHER.

The other words for Informal Coaching are corridor coaching, coaching on the fly, impromptu coaching, intuitive coaching, and 'coaching on the go.' You may also call it a 'coaching moment.'

Leaders who master Speed coaching use a simple dialogue process that helps individuals tap into their innate reflection, critical thinking, and problem-solving capabilities. It is a method to gently engage others through inquiry, encouraging them to reflect more and broaden their understanding of themselves and their unique abilities.

My definition of Speed Coaching is "A 'coach-like leader' acts as an accountability partner to empower the team to choose and follow their success path responsibly to unleash their full potential"

I am presenting the critical distinctions between formal and informal coaching.

DIMENSION	FORMAL COACHING	INFORMAL COACHING
Format	Structured	Unstructured
Schedules	Pre-decided	Spontaneous
Duration	60-90 minutes	3-5 minutes
Contract	Agreed by both Coach & Coachee	Coachee may not even know
Setting	Professional	Corridor, hallway
Pre-Coaching	Assessment tools	No assessment tools
Who does the coaching?	Done by a certified professional coach	Part of the line manager's daily role
Frequency	Once or twice a month, 10-12 sessions a year	Almost daily
Focus of coaching	Growth and career development needs	More urgent, short-term, reactive needs challenges

THREE SIGNS OF A COACHING OPPORTUNITY

I am writing this chapter with the purpose of helping leaders understand the following:

How to spot a speed coaching opportunity. It might be a waste if you didn't know it was a coaching moment. That means you missed the chance to grow someone's potential.

Remember, leadership happens in small daily conversations— one conversation at a time. What happens in that one conversation determines your leadership impact.

How does the person you interact with leave the meeting? Energized, motivated, and ready to take action with full ownership? Or dismayed, dejected, demotivated, prepared to invent some justification for non-action?

You must also understand that only some interactions call for a coaching conversation. There are situations where you need to use other management tools, styles, and development methods to achieve the desired outcomes.

Leaders require a powerful formula to help them decide when to turn on the coaching mode. They need to learn between managing and coaching moments and be in the coaching zone. Get ready to learn the formula.

SIGN #1:

AREA

The first question I ask leaders is this:

Is the area of discussion, topic, or situation a coachable opportunity?

Let me give you a million-dollar insight.

Imagine someone from your team brings a problem to you, and they ask for a solution.

If, as a leader, you feel the urge to give an answer or resolve the issue, it means this is a clear speed coaching opportunity. Your very temptation to quickly offer the solution is a sign of a coaching moment. Desire to give your expert advice is an excellent indicator to explore the possibility of coaching rather than problem-solving.

> **A simple assessment is to gauge whether the Coachee's issue involves a known, clear, and correct solution.**

If the problem Coachee brings has only one correct solution, and only you have that, it is not a speed coaching opportunity. Speed coaching only works when there is more than one possible solution to a problem. Therefore, it is an excellent opportunity to engage your team in an insightful conversation and let them explore their answers.

Your job is to build self-realization, opening doors to new insights, so they see issues from multiple perspectives. Your questions will allow them to think out of the box. They may or may not come up with the perfect solution. And later on, you may also affirm that your answer was the best. But it doesn't matter.

> Sometimes, the purpose of speed coaching is not to solve a problem but stretch their minds. It engages them in a constructive dialogue. A conversation that makes them feel listened to. An interaction that helps them understand that they can think strategically and that their views also matter.

When leaders run this exercise daily, they report to us that their teams have started showing up more prepared. They love being asked insightful questions. They wait for the opportunity to show the leaders how intelligent they are and what homework they have already done for the issue.

On the contrary, if leaders fail to read the first sign of engaging teams in speed coaching, they give opinions and solutions. Result? It undermines the conversation. Coachee feels disempowered, and their ownership and self-accountability drop down. Their ability to resolve the problem still needs to be explored.

Advice-giving is quite natural to leaders, managers, and bosses. Why do they do that?

Advice-giving is a significant temptation for coaching leaders. This temptation is often driven by a habit and reinforced by its efficiency, which is to provide answers, opinions, and solutions.

There is nothing wrong apparently with advice-giving. After all, you are helping your team solve problems more quickly. These are wonderful attributes to have. However, in speed coaching, they sabotage the coaching conversation, leaving the Coachee without thinking for him or herself. The Coachee remains passive in the discussions. Mainly at the receiving end, they are not required to stretch their minds to find a solution.

SIGN #2:

TIMING

The second test of speed coaching is timing. The issue in hand can be a coaching moment; however, the timing may need to be corrected.

Fruitful coaching dialogue requires the right timing, place, and setting. You may prefer to discuss the issue in the presence of only a few people in the elevator. Or you are just about to enter an unavoidable meeting in a few seconds.

The Coachee needs to attend to something urgently, and they don't have a minute to continue the conversation. The issue may be so sensitive that you don't want to discuss it in front of another colleague sitting in your office.

What do you do when the timing is not correct?

You can make some adjustments to support coaching. For example, take a hallway conversation back to a private office or meeting space in a few minutes.

However, here is a secret point. Never leave the Coachee without a question to reflect on.

SIGN #3:

MOOD

What is the Coachee's emotional and mental state?

Caution: Emotionally overwhelmed 'brain fried' Coachee:

Establish the groundwork:

If not, can a meeting time be scheduled for the near future?

STEPPING INTO COACHING

That sounds like a lot, and I want to have all the facts correct. Can I ask you a few questions to clarify the issue?

This is a thought-provoking situation. Why don't we sit down and think this through together?

This is a complex issue; let's take a walk and get some coffee so I can hear more. Do you have five minutes to go to the cafeteria together?

Always start by asking one or two clarifying questions and then default to the typical strategy of giving solutions or input.

Gently transform a conversation from one where the leader is giving answers to one where the field is open to dialogue.

Over time, start with three or four questions before defaulting back. Eventually, start with five or six questions. Gradually introduce and change the methodology to one of coaching to make the interactions more "normal" to the Coachee.

How can I support you in taking on this challenge?

If you had to resolve this issue on your own, what might you do?

Given the problem you have described, what have you tried so far, or do you have any ideas you could try?

FOCUS

Develop opening lines that invite coaching.

Set expectations for yourself and those around you.

Make it a norm that you routinely ask questions and seek clarity.

'But I have already made it clear to my team that problems they present to me should also be accompanied by at least one idea for a solution.' A manager told me in one of my recent workshops.

Here are my thoughts on this:

'Telling people to always show up with a solution doesn't work. It's demanding an explanation, putting them under pressure to find the answer. However, when you speed coach, you use your skills to craft a robust conversation with them. The solution automatically arrives when they are asked the right questions at the right time.

When you believe in their potential and listen to their ideas by offering a chance to them to expand on their thinking. Throwing them in isolation and expecting them to bring a solution is not coaching. In speed coaching, you co-create a settlement with them.

A fascinating aspect of the coaching process is that it makes them believe it was their idea. They leave the interaction energized, taking full ownership to execute their solution.'

CAUTION

Applying coaching skills can initially take much work.

Employees and colleagues can spot the change in typical ways of interacting with them.

TRAP: Wanting to offer advice is the stickiest trap for many coaches early in their development.

APPLICATION

1. Goal setting
2. Strategic planning
3. Creating engagement
4. Motivating and inspiring
5. Delegating
6. Team-working
7. Problem-solving
8. Planning and reviewing
9. Team and people development
10. Career development
11. Performance management
12. Performance reviews
13. Feedback and appraisals
14. Relationship alignment

SPOTTING A COACHING CONVERSATION

How would you know that the conversation you had with your team was a coaching conversation?

FOCUS WAS ON THEM
The entire focus, attention, and importance were put on the Coachee during the conversation.

1. DECISIVE MOMENT

The Coachee admits that they would likely have that learning with this conversation.

2. IMPACT:

There was a significant change in Coachee's understanding, learning, and behavior. Also, the Coachee reports notable progress as a result of that conversation.

SPEED COACHING TIP

1. Remember, only some coaching conversations will produce the desired impact. Don't get disappointed. The key is to keep practicing.
2. Action may not occur in the first conversation. Follow through on your conversations is vital.

COMMAND AND CONTROL MANAGERS	COACH-LIKE LEADERS
Command and control managers assume that others:	Coaching leaders, on the other hand, believe that people:
1. Have a genuine distaste for work	1. Want to work because working is natural
2. Must be prodded or threatened into work because it is so unpleasant	2. Will exercise self-control if they are committed to the results to be achieved
3. Prefer to be closely supervised	3. They will be motivated to achieve goals if they value their goals.
4. Avoid as much responsibility as they can	4. 4. Share imagination and creativity – traits not limited solely to management.
5. Value security above all else.	5. Are "boxed in" by job descriptions and are capable of realizing more potential than they are typically given a chance to do

Chapter 06

★ **Core Coaching Skills
to Speed Coach**

Core Coaching Skills
to Speed Coach

Coaching is a skill in demand. According to the International Coach Federation, employees who receive coaching report significant increases in engagement, retention, and collaboration.

Coaching multiplies your effectiveness as a manager. Having coaching skills means you will grow exponentially as a leader. When you apply for a new job, a coaching certification on your portfolio distinguishes you from other candidates. Organizations also value managers who can coach and expect them to grow leaders around them. Coaching skills allow you as a leader to connect with your team, build deeper rapport and trust and achieve results beyond expectations.

At the heart of coaching, there are two skills. Listening and questioning. There could be many others, but these two are at the core. To me, listening tops the two. It is not possible to ask a quality question without demonstrating effective listening. Because your next question doesn't stem from your memory, it comes from better listening to Coachee's perspectives, challenges, and beliefs.

> **Real listening is about understanding the Coachee's perspective and opening the gateway to their world.**

Becoming a coach allows you to develop the skills believed to be rare in this fast-paced business world. However, for coaches, all these skills come naturally. Coaching is a decision. Once you choose to operate from a coaching position, you naturally surround yourself with the intent and opportunity to harness these skills. Let's commit to some gruelling workouts to develop these core skills.

Skill #1:

LISTENING

Listening sounds simple, but it is not, and it is challenging to acquire. We all overestimate our ability to listen. Most of the leaders believe they are above-average listeners. In reality, they are not.

In a study, it was noticed that doctors interrupt their patients while they speak every 18th seconds. Similar studies found that corporate leaders outperform doctors by interrupting their team members every 11th second.

> *Bosses only hear. Leaders demonstrate listening*

REFLECT

Before providing leaders with tools to improve their listening, we encourage them to raise their self-awareness (and insight). The exercise below will help you become more conscious of how you typically listen.

Today, as you go about your day, use your conversations to consider the following:

Q. *How often do you pretend to listen to someone but don't?*

Q. *How is your listening different within different circumstances or with various people?*

Q. *What effect does the quality of your listening seem to have on other people or the conversation?*

LEVELS OF LISTENING

Different leaders are at varying levels of listening ability. Our structured observations revealed five listening levels leaders demonstrate in daily conversations with their teams.

I want you to be brutally honest and spot the daily level you see yourself operating at.

Level #1:
Waiting for your turn

Coachee: I need some clarification. I am still trying to figure out what to do.

Leader: You won't believe what happened in the meeting I have just been to ....

Level #2:
Giving your own experience

Coachee: Can you please help me decide which training course I should take?
Leader: Let me tell you about the last leadership course I went to. What happened was ....

Level #3:
Giving advice

Coachee: I am having trouble dealing with the accounts guy
Leader: What you need to do is talk to write him an email copying his boss ....

Level #4:
Listening and asking for more
Coachee: I am completely overwhelmed with this workload. I need to figure out where to start.
Leader: Tell me more about that

Level #5:
Deep listening

Coachee: I didn't get the promotion and I am no longer interested.
Leader: Are you seriously not interested, or is something else bothering you?

Leadership happens in daily conversations. One conversation at a time. It is so essential for leaders to develop awareness about their impact in these conversations. As a leader, are you making people feel good about themselves (and you) in daily interactions with you?

> **I take leaders through various listening exercises
> in my Speed Coaching training sessions.**

In my recent training, I asked participants to pair up with a partner in the audience. They were told that one partner would leave the room, recall an interesting life incident, and develop a three-minute story to share with their partners.

The other group of partners stayed with me in the room. They were instructed to demonstrate total listening for the first 60 seconds. And then, for the next 30 seconds, they will perform all kinds of conversation-killers, i.e., seeing their phones, looking around, breaking eye contact, yawning, and showing no interest in the person or the story.

The first group was called back into the room to share their stories. Both groups did what they were told to do.

I ask the storytellers to share their experiences. They invariably started with the first phase, where they were wholly listened to, and the other person demonstrated a level-5 listening.

The most frequently expressed feelings were, I felt ……….

- Respected
- Valued
- Important
- Confident
- Trusted

And then, the participants recalled their experience from the second phase. Without exception, participants described their feeling using the following expressions: I felt ………

- Degraded
- Angry
- Hurt
- Disrespected
- Not valued
- Useless and unimportant

The beauty was that this happened with the same person within less than three minutes. Recall a recent conversation with your colleague who directly reports to you. This should be a conversation that you initiated. Try recollecting every detail of the interaction and assess the quality of your listening skills.

1. Whose agenda did you follow?
2. Did you give advice?
3. What do you think the other person felt while leaving your desk?

When someone next time asks to discuss something with you, try listening actively to them. In your future interactions with your colleagues, assess yourself after every conversation using the following questions:

1. Did you stay on their agenda?
2. Did you suspend judgment?
3. Did you clarify and reflect on what they said?
4. Did you hold back your opinion or advice?
5. Did you help your colleague explore their thoughts?
6. Did you use your intuition?
7. What are you learning about your listening skills?
8. What area of listening do you choose to focus on to develop further?

Quality of listening is the driving factor in the quality of conversation.

CASE STUDY

Saif, the director of a well-regarded non-profit organization, has a solid national reputation for his knowledge and track record of successful advocacy. Though his external partners, grantees, and funders appreciate his work ethic, contacts, and influence on a national stage, the staff needs help to follow him.

They perceive him as arrogant, uncaring, and at times downright rude. The problem lies primarily in his need for more ability to listen. When employees enter his office, he is typically typing on his computer or phone and is busy working. But Saif continues when people are present. When co-workers attempt to converse with him, he is often inattentive to their needs.

Saera, a project lead and high performer in the team, describes her interactions with Saif this way: *"When I go into his office, he rarely will look up from what he is doing. Or if he does look up, it's only briefly to say hello. It feels like he isn't interested in my situation, and I have to repeat myself many times during the conversation. It makes me not want to talk anymore, and I certainly avoid dealing with him as much as possible. He makes me feel like I am a nuisance and a bother. I love my work but wish to report to someone else."*

The deputy director, Maddy refers to him *as 'unintentional but damaging.'*

'He does not realize how everyone perceives him. I tried talking to him about it, but he typically dismisses the critique by claiming he is busy. He says multitasking is a common part of work; everyone should understand. We have lost some good people because they have grown tired of his neglect."

The harder Saif works, cramming as much as he can into the workday, constantly doing two things at once, the more he isolates himself from the team.

Here are a few questions for you to reflect on:

1. Did the situation sound familiar to you?
2. If you were on Saif's team, what would you feel about yourself and him?
3. What is causing Saif to behave this way?
4. What will be the consequences for Saif if he doesn't change?
5. What advice would you like to give to Saif?

SIGNS OF SUPER LISTENING

In our Speed Coaching training programs, I teach leaders my *'Super'* listening formula. This five-step process is a no-fail tool to demonstrate power listening.

Sign #1: **You Summarize**

You listen carefully to every bone of your body and then *summarize* what you think your direct report has said. You repeat back briefly, without changing the substance or meaning.

Leaders report to me that this tool is magic. When they summarise, their team members feel stunned.

One leader in the post-training follow-up session said excitedly, 'They couldn't believe I was listening. Not only did they get this clear sign that I was all ears for them, but also it helped me clarify and double-check my understanding of their viewpoint.'

Sign #2: **You Don't Interrupt**

The best gift you can give someone is the gift of listening. Typically, we jump at the first opportunity to interrupt.

Interruptions occur because we are impatient and need the stamina to listen. We want to fill in the blanks, throw judgments, and impose our views.

I have witnessed hundreds of leaders interacting with their teams. Leaders are usually in a hurry. They think they don't have time. Therefore, they quickly try to conclude every interaction. This desire pushes them to interrupt people. Their teams feel frustrated when they are not permitted to finish their sentences.

Employees feel valued and important when leaders allow their teams to finish their part of the conversation. If you want to make someone's day today, give them an uninterrupted chance to talk.

Sign #3: **You Let Them Expand**

Providing someone the space to expand on what they were saying is exceptional. This, indeed, is the highest form of listening.

Not only did you not interrupt your direct report (requires volumes of patience, though), but once your colleague finished, you either stayed silent, giving them a clear clue to continue speaking, or you asked a brief question like 'What else,' and the person resumed the speaking role.

When leaders encourage others to speak more, they listen to what they never hear. People begin to share their deepest concerns, worries, and actual obstacles.

Especially when someone presents an idea and leaders offer them a chance to expand, their teams feel that their opinions are heard and valued.

Sign #4: **100% Eye Contact**

Maintaining eye contact is the most accessible signal leaders can give their team to demonstrate listening. Remember when someone gave you complete focus, maintained eye contact with you, and appeared they forgot even to blink their eyes? Recollect that feeling.

Isn't it a treat to be with someone who dedicates their complete attention to you? When leaders maintain engaging eye contact, it increases their presence. Also, it gives your team the impression that, at this moment, nothing matters more than this conversation to you in this world.

Sign #5: **You Reflect Back**

Reflecting is repeating some of those keywords and phrases your team member used in the conversation. It has two advantages:
One, it shows you are fully engaged in the dialogue.
Two, it allows your Coachee to reflect on what they have just said.

Coachee: I am feeling frustrated because of the constant delay from the suppliers.
Leader: So, you feel frustrated.

 Super listening encourages self-expression, builds trust, develops intimacy, and nurtures openness. Here's a quick summary of SUPER listening for you:

- Summarize to check the viewpoint.
- Uninterrupted chances to talk
- Providing space to expand

- Eye contact - complete focus on them
- Reflect to confirm & show engagement

ADDITIONAL LISTENING TOOLS:

1. **Paraphrasing:**
   Using slightly different word(s) which do not change the substance or meaning of what the other person said.

2. **Clarifying:**
   Expressing succinctly the essence/core of what has been said and adding something valuable picked up intuitively from emotions or discrepancies in words or expressions of face or body that haven't been told in words to generate insight and clarity for the speaker and check that you understood: "It sounds like ....What would you say?"

3. **Suspending judgment & criticism**
   Keeping an open mind. Judgments and criticism make people defensive and stop them from talking.

4. **Mirroring-back**
   This is another powerful technique that I teach my certified/professional/full-time coaches only. However, I have incorporated this in my recent Speed Coaching programs also.

 Coach-leaders who master mirroring-back report that their teams feel fully heard. They understand that mirroring back is not parroting back. Mirroring-back helps Coachee's explore and express their thought process. Mirroring-back shows that you are listening with intent and allows coach-leaders to pay attention to body movements, gestures, tone of voice, speech pacing, pauses, and eye movements.

TWO RARE ABILITIES:

Besides, leaders must develop two additional abilities to listen at a higher level.

One is *listening for potential*. It means focusing on capabilities and strengths rather than past performance or seeing someone as a problem. What could the person unleash if there were no limits?

And the second level is *listening with heart* and to non-verbal messages such as voice tone, phrasing, facial expression, and body language. Listen attentively at the level of feeling and meaning (the intent) to hear the core/ essence of what is being conveyed.

THE LISTENING CAP FORMULA

In our practice sessions with leaders, we have observed that using CAP Formula (*confirm, acknowledge, presence*) dramatically improves their impact and listening skills. Here is the formula:

Rule #1:
CONFIRM: *Let me confirm my understanding*

During coaching dialogues, leaders who use the following phrases are consistently rated as great listeners:

- Is part of what you are saying is….?
- I sense a bit of disconnect between you and your boss on this issue. Is that correct?
- You feel more committed to the planning part. Have I understood this right?
- You appear to be satisfied with the outcomes. Have I picked this up correctly? If not, how would you describe this?

Rule #2:
ACKNOWLEDGE: *I want to understand your words.*

Instead of assuming what the person has said, coach-leaders take a pause and ask these clarifying questions.

1. What I hear you saying is ….
2. What I heard was ….
3. So you want to move ahead on this …

Rule #3:
PRESENCE: *I am right here with you*

The coaching leaders graduate to a higher degree of listening when they pick up the Coachee's words and turn them into questions:

Coachee: I should focus more on my team's development.
Coach: 'How will focusing more on team development help you achieve your sales targets?
Coachee: This is the right time to invest in this new venture.
Coach: What will be the impact of investing in this new venture?

Imagine, as a leader, you are using the CAP formula with your team. If you ask someone to record this conversation, you will see yourself doing the following in that film.

1. You are lucid and fully present with the person speaking to you
2. Your awareness is entirely focused on the other person
3. Your mind is mostly quiet and calm
4. You have a reduced sense of yourself

Peter Drucker says, 'listening is not a skill. It's a discipline.' Unfortunately, most leaders today do not live up to this discipline.

Most leaders in today's super-busy world have embraced a particular disease, Split Attention Disorder [SAD]. Very sad indeed. They seem to be distracted, in a rush not able to concentrate.

When leaders do not demonstrate effective listening, their teams perceive that they are disinterested or don't care. Their teams go into their shells and stop giving them feedback or input for improvement.

Leaders need to be fully aware of the damage of not listening. Not only does your team become less engaged, but lack of listening drastically reduces your attention, focus, and awareness also.

Listening is a moment-to-moment choice. Listening it is a decision. Great coach-leaders master the art of listening. They listen to the content and what is behind the words.

Improved listening produces a measurable impact on your team's self-motivation and ownership. Your team begins to realize that you don't listen to reply, and you instead listen to understand.

Skill #2:

POWER QUESTIONING

"Coaching is an art, and it's far easier said than done. It takes courage to ask a question rather than offer advice, provide an answer, or unleash a solution. Giving another person the opportunity to find their own way, make their own mistakes, and create their wisdom is both brave and vulnerable.

-**Brené Brown**, author of *Rising Strong and Daring Greatly*

Coaching is not about imposing our thinking and ideas on others; coaching is stimulating a thought process in the mind of the Coachee so that they can create their own conclusions.

Go and try throwing a stone in the middle of a lake. Now stop and watch. That tiny stone will create a jolt inside the lake. Not much is apparent from the outside. It produces circles around the place you threw that small rock. However, within seconds it starts expanding the circles. Those circles move to the outside towards the bank. Until they hit the shore, they do not stop.

POWER OF POWER QUESTIONS

Questions play the same role in the coaching process—straightforward clarification and common questions cannot create that ripple effect. If you ask a question and the person instantly responds without thinking, it is not a power question.

If you ask a question and the Coachee goes silent. Waits to respond. Engages in thinking and reflecting. This is a sign that the question was powerful. It hit the Coachee's thought lake differently and created a ripple effect. Now the Coachee is silent, accessing their deepest thoughts and emotions, finding an answer that they never tried finding before.

> Why do we ask questions? Why can we not simply share our views when we are so confident? After all, we have experience, and the Coachee does not. Why cannot we plant the answer in their mind?

Many leaders resist coaching using such questions as an excuse.

My response is simple.

> **'Our personal views can reduce Coachee's ability to find their answers. Instead of planning a response, we must strive to plant a seed of thinking, reflecting, and self-awareness that eventually leads the Coachee to act more responsibly.**

Like our kids, we own our ideas. They are very dear to us. When people are encouraged to give solutions, they do—provided you give them safety. They go the extra mile to prove their idea is superior. They will persist more in the face of failure and handle the disappointments themselves.

During the first wave of Covid, the head of our coaching division spoke to me about one of our top clients who had registered seven of their executives in our Global Coach Certification Program. Due to the Covid-19 and subsequent lockdown, we were thinking to postpone the program. She wanted my *advice* on how to respond to the client.

Like everyone, I jumped to the solution, thinking I had the best one.

 'Let us convert them to our online program.' I said it because many clients had already done that.

'That won't be possible because the client has categorically told me they will not attend the online program.' She said pretty assertively.

I immediately realized I had made a mistake here. I did not use the ATM formula. Like many leaders, I thought, offering the advice here would save time. But it turned out that she knew far more about the client than I did.

'So, knowing what you know about the client, what do you recommend?' I finally asked a coaching question.

With a confident tone of voice, she told me what she thought would be the next best option.

'What makes you confident that the client will accept this proposal?'. That was my next question.

She started giving me all the logical reasons based on her understanding of the client's needs and situation that only she knew.

'Go ahead.' I said.

She concluded the call with a big smile and a sense of victory, and that was precisely what I wanted.

Later, she texted me to confirm that the client had accepted her proposal.

If I had tried imposing my solution, she would have least bought in. She would have returned to me informing me that your idea did not work.

'I knew it already,' she might say, 'but I didn't tell you because I didn't want to offend you.' I might have had to listen to such a statement if I were an insecure leader.

Creative questioning is at the heart of effective coaching. Asking the right question at the right time is central to coaching success. Questioning is a critical skill.

> **When leaders master questioning skill, they provoke a thought process that enables employees to assess the situation brand-newly.**

Asking a question is not limited to coaching; many professionals ask questions. Journalists, teachers, and FBI agents all use the power of questions.

The difference is the purpose. The purpose of asking a question in coaching is different. Coaching leaders do not ask questions to gather information, assess knowledge, interrogate or unmask some hidden truth, or publicly embarrass the person.

Here the purpose is to build self-awareness. To instill an insight. To sow the seed of a new perspective. To open a new window of possibility. To bring something into the limelight for the person that might have been hidden in the backyard.

Coach-leaders do not need that information. They want the Coachee to build responsibility around their choices.

Expert coaching leaders ask questions not to get an answer they want to hear but to encourage meaningful thoughts that can help the other person address a challenge or break through to a new level of performance.

> **Unlike mentoring, in which the leader may share personal experiences and provide advice, while asking questions with a coaching mindset, the goal is to help the person uncover that insight themselves.**

Leaders ask questions to create the space for those "aha!" moments. Telling them what to do deprives them of this moment of discovery. True leaders know that it will be better for the Coachee if they reach that insight themselves instead of feeling it was told to them by someone.

We all value our ideas and conclusions much more than we do others.

QUESTIONS:

 Managers may think they are asking a question when they actually are disguising an instruction:

"Don't you think it is good to go with option A?"

By contrast, open questions such as *"What do you see as a way forward?"* allows a team member to come up with their answer. It is also important to encourage feedback on one's coaching skills and take the time to reflect on this.

WHAT QUESTIONS DO YOU HAVE?

The quality of your coaching is the quality of your questions. Here is what happens when you ask powerful coaching questions.

TRIGGER QUESTIONS	EXAMPLE
Trigger thoughts	What is your definition of a healthy, positive relationship?
Require answer	Did you get a chance to see the President?
Increase self-awareness	What are your top three priorities in life?
Gain involvement & commitment.	How are you going to make sure that you put this plan to action?
Generate solutions	What options do you have? What if you had all the resources?
Encourage evaluation, re-evaluation, and quality feedback	What makes you do that? What are your thoughts now?
Reinforce responsibility to act and initiate change	What will it take for you to make it happen?

Questions create both awareness and responsibility.

1. Inspire creativity and resourcefulness.
2. Increase possibilities/vision.
3. Build goal orientation
4. Encourage solution focus
5. Help you stay non-judgmental
6. Facilitate attention, thoughts, and observation
7. Create a higher degree of focus, detail, and precision
8. Surface quality of thoughts, performance, and thinking
9. Support, challenge, and motivate

COACHING QUESTIONS:

Questions are magic, because they…..

1. Follow the interest of the Coachee.
2. Compel attention
3. Help learn, grow, and succeed
4. Increase self-belief and motivation
5. Evoke clarity
6. Focus for precision
7. Create a feedback loop

ADVICE	QUESTION
Incorrect:	Correct:
You should take this feedback seriously and do what I say	How are you going to respond to the feedback?

PURPOSE OF COACHING QUESTIONS:

Coach-like leaders don't ask questions because they need to collect information. They are not CIA agents, journalists, or class teachers. They ask questions because they want to raise the self-awareness of the Coachee. The coach-leader needs to know that the Coachee has the correct information and has full awareness of the situation.

COUNTERPRODUCTIVE QUESTIONS:

 Any question that starts with 'Why' can be counterproductive for the coaching process. The reason is that a 'why' question implies criticism. A why question evokes defensiveness. Try asking someone today, 'Why did you do that'? And see the person becoming defensive.

Why questions put the Coachee in analysis mode, which is the opposite of self-awareness. Why questions trigger analytical thinking, which is opposite to raising self-awareness, the foundation of the coaching process.

The purpose of any coaching conversation is to encourage observation, reflection, and self-realization. Analysis and awareness are two different mental models that cannot operate simultaneously. So what do you replace why question with? The answer is a 'How' question. See the comparison below:

WHY QUESTION	HOW QUESTION
Why did you do that?	How will you do that?
What are the reasons?	What are the steps?

OPEN QUESTIONS

1. What do you want to achieve?
2. What is happening now?
3. How would you like it to be?
4. Where would you find out more?
5. What will you do?

With the goal of your conversation established, ask questions rooted in what, when, where, and who, each of which force people to come down out of the clouds and focus on specific facts.

This makes the conversation honest and constructive. You'll notice that we didn't include why. That's because asking why demands people explore reasons and motivations rather than facts. In doing that, it can carry overtones of judgment or trigger attempts at self-justification, both of which can be counterproductive.

As a leader, when you are required to challenge Coachee's beliefs, opinions, and fixed mindsets, you can use the following questions:

1. What makes you say that?
2. What if that is not true?
3. What will you do if you have no fear?
4. if that is not a problem, what will you do?

SEVEN POWER QUESTIONS

This question bag consists of my top seven — a list of simple yet profound questions you can have at your fingertips.

1. If I were not here, what would you do? (My all-time favorite question, which I use to prove to the cynical that coaching does not take time, it takes one powerful question!)
2. If you knew the answer, what would it be? (Not as tough as it sounds since it enables the Coachee to look beyond the blockage.) If you did know? (In response to "I don't know")
3. What if there are no limits?
4. What advice would you give to a friend in your situation?
5. Imagine having a dialogue with the wisest you know or can think of. What would they tell you to do?
6. What else? (This used at the end of most answers will evoke more.
7. What is your commitment to doing it on a scale of 1-10? What can you do to make it a 10?

The proper use of the Socratic Method and open-ended questioning are skills that leaders should always possess. They effectively allow a team to utilize their strengths to benefit the organization. Open-ended questions expand perspective.

 Active listening is a critical coaching skill possessed by competent managers and leaders. Being able to fully understand your team's message and the emotional connection behind their message enables a leader to improve communication. This is a powerful skill to connect with others in every area of life.

With more and more organizations embracing coaching as a way of managing, these skills are being perfected and taught worldwide. All the tools working together can create higher functioning on all levels. Mindful leaders make a change, and aware leaders have practical coaching skills.

A manager with practical coaching skills does not give orders. The collaboration will be valued over control in a well-coached organization. The more the team actively engaged in moving forward, the better that team will perform.

Healthy stress builds skills and confidence, whereas excess pressure builds distress. Refrain from whipping your team. Employees respect a hard-working leader rather than being afraid of a fear-mongering leader. Leading by example is incredibly important in an organization.

EXAMPLES OF COACHING SKILLS IN ACTION

An employee needs to be consistently on time and underperforming at the employee's job. A manager has noticed this reduction in productivity. Rather than creating fear in this situation, a competent manager will dial-up empathy and collaborate with active listening in a critical evaluation conversation. Illuminating this employee on how using personal strengths can help the employee overcome whatever obstacle is faced will help improve productivity.

When facing a crisis, which is subjectively defined, a skilled manager approaches it with a cool head. Asking for ideas from all team members to "fix" the situation will generate more ideas than trying to solve it individually. A manager with practical coaching skills can approach any obstacle with a calm, objective focus. A deeper understanding of problems and solution-focused questioning creates pathways to resolutions.

A new employee visibly nervous about their new role is linked with another professional by a manager. The two are encouraged to set goals together and to hold each other accountable. This coaching skill would enable a team to collaborate and create a social connection to build community within the organization.

There is a conflict between two employees. The practical coaching skills of active, equal listening and emotional intelligence are used to reduce anger, stress, and ineffective communication. Allowing space for each party in the conflict to be heard and co-create solutions helps unify the team.

Developing your coaching skills will take effort. It is like a self-development journey, for any growth requires effort.

WHEN TO COACH?

1. When you assign tasks to your team members.
2. When you are supposed to give feedback to one of your direct reports.
3. When you are bringing new employees on board.
4. When your team member tries to give their monkeys away.
5. When you are helping others overcome setbacks or challenges
6. When you are having a performance appraisal conversation
7. When you deal with an employee having a performance problem
8. When you want your direct reports to develop skills and abilities
9. When you are creating a career path for your direct reports
10. When you converse with an employee who has failed to do something "right."
11. When an employee wants help or guidance from you.
12. When your team members need a sounding board or want to vent

Stage 03

APPLY
Coaching Frameworks at the Workplace

Chapter #7 – Conversational Framework for Speed Coaching
- Direction
- Analysis
- Roadmap
- Empower

Chapter #8 – Foundation of a Coaching Relationship
- Trust
- Respect
- Rapport

Chapter 07

**Framework for
Coaching Conversations**

Framework for Coaching Conversations

Coaching is a conversation between two equal individuals. The structure is one critical element differentiating coaching conversations from managers' routine interactions with their direct reports.

Having a structure allows the leaders to strike the right balance between keeping the conversation flowing naturally and focusing on the core outcome.

Coaching with a tested framework can produce the desired results. However, coach-leaders must understand that coaching is a 'process' rather than a 'model.' You cannot produce results through coaching by asking seven (pre-conceived) questions and tick-boxing four steps.

A coach-leader must be flexible while moving the conversation toward action through a robust coaching framework.

DARE COACHING MODEL

Here is the Speed Coaching Conversational Framework to bring the conversation alive and produce impact. World's #1 Leadership Coach, Marshall Goldsmith, has endorsed the DARE™ Coaching Model. Let me take you through a step-by-step process to understand the model.

STAGE #1
DIRECTION
WHAT DO YOU WANT?

STAGE #4
EMPOWER
WHAT WILL YOU DO?

STAGE #2
ANALYSIS
WHAT'S HAPPENING NOW?

STAGE #3
ROADMAP
WHAT COULD YOU DO?

Stage #1: **DIRECTION:**

At the onset of every Speed-Coaching opportunity, coaching leaders clarify the exact outcome the Coachee would like to achieve at the end of that short conversation.

No coaching exchange will occur until both leader and the Coachee agree on the desired results expected from the interaction. Influential coaching leaders dare ask this question at the start of the speed coaching session,

"What do you want to achieve when you walk out the door that you don't have now?"

Stage #2: **ANALYSIS**

To help the Coachee move toward the agreed direction, the leader and the Coachee need to analyze exactly where they are compared to where they want to be. Master leader-coaches help Coachees see through the fog with

objectivity and see the current reality. Leader-coach at this stage asks analysis-focused questions to uncover what is happening.

A good question at this point would be, *"What are the key things we need to know?"*

At this stage, as a leader, you need to explore the roadblocks of the Coachee. You will determine what behaviors, perceptions, habits, or attitudes must be changed. When coach-like leaders listen carefully, they determine whether the Coachee is stuck with the technical or human side.

Leaders who practice this style later on, report to us that when instead of blaming, judging, or advising, we engage people in non-threatening conversations, they connect with the deeper side of themselves. Their ability to reflect empowers them to see things in a brand-new way. They start accessing their own insights and committing to solving their problem.

When leaders invest time in this stage, the conversation automatically flows into the coaching process.

Stage #3: **ROADMAP**

In our post-training sessions on Speed Coaching, most leaders reported that their direct reports, at the beginning of most coaching conversations, helplessly stated that they had no idea about what to do with the problem at hand. They felt utterly stuck. They thought they could do nothing to handle the situation. At this stage of the conversation, your job as a leader-coach is to deepen and widen the exchange.

One of my favorite questions to expand their thinking beyond the current problem is to ask, "If you had a magic wand, what would you do?"

I have seen people going unstoppable. You will be surprised to know that the person who, a minute ago, was clueless and claimed to be stuck and have no solutions begins to generate power solutions. They seem to start thinking anew.

At the same time, good coach-leaders remember to help them go deep by evaluating the consequences, drawbacks, and risks of going to the solutions they proposed.

Stage #4: **EMPOWER**

 This stage is the cornerstone of the whole coaching process. The key question here for you as a coach-leader is. *'What do you think the Coachee will do about the issue at hand'?*

Of all the possible actions both of you explored together, which one is the Coachee committing to taking? What is the likelihood that the Coachee will take those actions? What problems can obstacle their path to taking action?

Leader-coach at this stage establishes accountability with the Coachee. The leader's job here is to ensure that the Coachee will follow through on their commitment.

HOW TO APPLY DARE™ COACHING FRAMEWORK

DARE™ Coaching Model creates magical conversations. The leaders who apply this framework report a powerful impact in their daily conversations. Here are the application guide and power questions to help you bring new life to your professional interactions with your direct reports. This model is applicable in both conversations initiated by you or your team.

Application
Stage #1: DIRECTION

Right from the start of the conversation, it is the responsibility of the coach-leader to set the direction and know where the discussion should be heading.

To set the *'Direction'* of the speed-coaching, a leader-coach will use the following questions with their direct report (Coachee):

1. What would you like to achieve in this conversation?
2. What would make this time well spent for you?
3. What would be the most helpful thing for you to take away at the end of our conversation?
4. What is the desired result for you of this conversation?

If the person is confused or brings more than one issues into the conversation, you can ask, *'It sounds like you have two goals. What would you like to focus on first?'* or *'Viewing those goals, what would you like to focus on in this conversation?'*

Also, as a leader, you would like to see whether or not the Coachee understands the true significance of the task. Here, you can ask this question: *'What will that enable you to do?'* or *'What will you have that you don't have now?'*

To develop greater clarity, the following questions can also be helpful:

1. Imagine, its three months from now and all obstacles have been removed allowing you to achieve your goal. What will you see, feel and hear?
2. 'How would you like it to be? *(How important is that to you?)*

When Coachee reflects on what they want by the end of the conversation, they force them to get to the *core point.*

When they know what they want to walk away with at the end of those five minutes, they become more serious and focused on the interaction. So always remember to ask, *'What would be the most helpful things to take away from this interaction?*

Application
Stage #2: ANALYSIS

As a leader-coach, you can only apply the Speed Coaching methodology once you know what is happening or what the present situation looks like.

Your purpose as a coach-leader is to identify what the person is doing that is getting in the way of their goals. What has stopped them from doing more? What internal resistance do they have to take action?

When leaders learn to master Speed Coaching, they don't look for answers at the surface level. They dig deeper. They explore on a scale of 1-10. If an ideal situation is 10, what number are they at now? What number do they like to be at? They also figure out the impact of the current situation on them and their work.

Coaching leaders' most important questions here would be:

1. What action(s) have you taken so far?
2. What resources do you already have (skill, time, enthusiasm, support, money, etc.)?
3. What other resources are needed?
4. What are you doing that takes you toward your goal?
5. What can you count on yourself for here?
6. What are you most / least confident about?
7. What is your main concern here?
8. How much control do you personally have over the outcome?

Knowing what is happening at the moment is not enough, leaders must understand what makes their team feel so sure about their assessment of the situation. Leaders who wear coaching shoes automatically dig out the obstacles their direct reports must overcome. They also identify what is helping or not helping.

Application
Stage #3: ROADMAP

 Instead of jumping into an advice-giving mode, coach-leaders pause and commit to surface the answers in their Coachee's mind. When you ask intelligent questions, you will know their current options and methods to get the result they want.

Your job as a coach-leader is to spot what ideas they have that might work here. What alternatives do they have? Which options would give them the best results? What appeals to them the most?

The following questions will help your Coachee illuminate the roadmap:

1. What would you do if you were the boss and had more time, budget, or resources?
2. What if you could start again with a clean sheet?
3. What has worked in the past? Who could help you with this?
4. What would you do if you had more time/control?
5. Whom do you know who would be good at this? What would they do?

One of my favorite questions that I use to help my Coachees build a quality roadmap is, *'What will be your advice to yourself?'*

Your role here is to challenge the Coachee to look for creative options to solve the problem. You will help them see what a permanent solution would look like. What could they do to avoid this happening again? What can they do to prevent or reduce this risk?

Application
Stage #4: EMPOWER

The best outcome of the 'Empower' stage in the DARE™ Coaching Model is to know which options would give the best results for your Coachee. Which solutions appeal to you the most?

The role of a coaching-leader is to build a sense of accountability in their Coachee's mind about the action they commit to taking. You may ask: *Which options do you choose? What are you going to do about it? So what will you do?*

Great leader-coach would explore the following answers to ensure full empowerment to their direct reports:

Which option appeals the most to you, feels suitable to you, and gives the best results?' Or

'How do you know this is going to work for you?'

Sometimes, your Coachee will commit to taking action and, after some time, will return, giving you justifications and excuses for not doing that. Good leader-coach will pre-empt this by asking this question:

1. When precisely are you going to start?
2. What stops you from starting earlier?
3. How committed are you to taking that action?
4. Is there anything you need to put in place before that?
5. What could happen to hinder you from taking this action?

Our Speed Coaching training programs encourage leaders to assess the support group around their direct reports to accomplish the agreed task. You can see the strength of their support network by asking this:

1. Who else needs to know what your plans are?
2. What support do you need? From whom?
3. What will you do to get that support?

Our research indicates that addressing the concerns like, *how you will do that, when you will do that, where you will go, whom you will talk to, or what is the first step*; gives both leaders and their reports the confidence to make desired actions happen. Many leaders find it helpful exploring what milestones they can identify or their timeframes to take the next steps. Coaching leaders also empower their teams by foreseeing how they would break this goal into smaller pieces.

Also, it is worth exploring if your Coachee is facing any personal resistance in taking these steps and what it will take for them to overcome this resistance. Empowerment will remain incomplete if leaders fail to ask the following two questions:

1. *What could I do to support you?*
2. *What could you do to support yourself?*

DARE™ COACHING MODEL IN ONE GLANCE

Stage	What to achieve at this stage?	Key Success Factors	role of Coach Leader
Stage 01: Direction	Where does the Coachee want to be? What is the issue at hand? What is the focus of this conversation?	Focus	Guide

Stage 02: Analysis	Where is the Coachee? What is holding them back? What obstacles do they need to overcome? What beliefs need to be changed and challenged?	Objectivity	Explore
Stage 03: Roadmap	What does the Coachee need to do to get there? What choices and options are available? What will a success plan look like? What are the critical milestones?	Choices	Challenge
Stage 04: Empower	How to make the Coachee accountable for the actions? How to spot and encourage progress? How do they sustain change? What long terms growth goals are they focusing on? What ongoing support might they need?	Accountability	Feedback & Follow Through

INSIGHTS

1. Coaching is a future-focused dialogue with a clear purpose of triggering action.
2. Coaching leaders use coaching to build the leadership skills of their team.
3. Leader-coach knows that the best way to develop someone's potential is to engage them in solving their own problems.

4. When leaders coach well, they help their teams develop their own processing, analysis, problem-solving, decision-making, and strategizing skills.

5. Good coaching leaders help their direct reports move from the current problem to the preferred future they want to create.

TRY ASKING THIS

- "What have you already thought of?"
- "What matters here?"

Pillars of a Coaching Relationship

Pillars of a Coaching Relationship

Coaching is not a technique or set of tools, and it's not a trick leaders can use to get things done through people. Coaching is a way of life, and coaching is a two-way relationship. For this relationship to grow, it needs to have a solid foundation.

After a decade-long research on the fundamentals of coaching, I have discovered three critical pillars of any successful coaching relationship. Here they are:

1. Trust
2. Respect
3. Rapport

Bosses have traditionally been dominating, intimidating, and even manipulating. Their core philosophy was to dominate their staff using the power of authority. They believed their survival was only possible if they were seen as a source of threat to their subordinates. Bosses mastered the art of manipulating to achieve whatever they wanted to achieve.

However, Coach-Like Leaders are a different breed. They believe coaching can only occur with trust, respect, and connection. The coaching style of leadership is rooted deep down in three fundamental human needs; trust, respect, and rapport. Coach-like leaders understand that:

1. There is no coaching if the person you coach doesn't trust you.
2. Coaching cannot be helpful if, as a leader, you did not earn respect from the person you are coaching.

3. Coaching is impossible without a certain degree of rapport between the leader-coach and the Coachee.

WHAT IS TRUST, RESPECT & RAPPORT?

Trust, respect, and rapport are all critical factors that can significantly impact a coaching conversation.

Trust means a person or organization is reliable and will act in one's best interest. Trust is essential in a coaching conversation because it allows team members to feel comfortable sharing personal information and discussing sensitive issues with their leader.

Respect refers to recognizing and accepting a person's inherent worth and dignity. Respect is essential in a coaching conversation because it allows team members to feel valued and appreciated by their leader.

Rapport is a positive relationship characterized by mutual understanding, trust, and respect. Rapport is essential in a coaching conversation because it creates a positive and productive environment where team members can communicate effectively with their leader.

A study in the Journal of Applied Psychology revealed that leader-member exchange (LMX) quality, including mutual trust and respect, positively relates to coaching effectiveness.

Bosses either don't feel the need or lack the ability to earn trust, respect, and rapport. However, when you decide to speed-coach and become a coach-like leader, you don't have a choice but start investing time and energy in establishing trust with your direct reports. You start giving them respect, and they begin to respect you enormously. You feel a different connection with them, leading to a deeper rapport with your team.

How will this respect, trust, and rapport thing impact workplace productivity? Phenomenally. You bet. People in your team will become unstoppable. For the first time, they will feel heard and valued. They will start enjoying work and feel excited instead of being dragged into it. They will start seeing you as a source of inspiration, not a threat.

WHY AM I SO CONFIDENT ABOUT THIS?

Because repeatedly, I have witnessed this transformation in dozens of organizations. People might have heard that leadership style can impact a direct report's performance by up to 70%. Now they start believing in it.

Leaders cannot just abruptly start coaching their teams. First, they have to meet the pre-coaching requirements and earn the right to become someone's coach. This change of hats drastically impacts the workplace culture. The idea of *'earning the right to coach'* is the real game changer.

Changing the team's perception of you would be the biggest challenge. However, when your team begins to see you as someone who believes in them, trusts them, respects them, listens to them, doesn't judge them, and sees potential in them instead of problems, it causes a significant shift in their perception of you. This shift in perception produces a major shift in your relationship with them and, eventually, a massive shift in the results you co-create with them.

This pre-coaching requisite provides the runway where coaching conversations can take off and help you and your direct reports soar to unimaginable heights.

When all the key leaders in the organization collectively make an effort to be more coach-like, the whole organization transforms. Cultural change becomes visible, and everyone feels leaders are doing something different. And that sounds amazing to everyone.

 The team notices the difference in leadership style. The new change is acknowledged and recognized by everyone.

That is why I strongly recommend that the whole leadership team go through the Speed Coaching training program together to make a dent and embed coaching as a vital part of the organization's DNA.

WHAT HAPPENS WHEN TRUST, RESPECT, AND RAPPORT ARE MISSING

 When trust, respect, and rapport are missing between a leader and their direct reports, it can hurt the quality of coaching conversations and the overall coaching culture in a company.

Without trust, respect, and rapport, team members are less inclined to share personal information or discuss sensitive issues with their leader, leading to poor communication and a lack of understanding of the team members' needs and concerns.

Having more engaged teams is a crucial desire of every leader. However, leaders must understand that they need to earn trust and respect if they want their teams to be invested in their goals. Failure to do so will result in low buy-in and decreased commitment to achieving results.

Our studies have revealed that trust and respect are necessary for team members to be more willing to take risks and try new things.

Many organizations struggle to hold employees accountable. But they never get to the root cause i.e. a lack of trust, respect, and rapport between the teams and leaders, without which it's not easier for leaders to hold the team accountable for their actions and decisions. Lack of confidence can cause weak and negative relationships, poor collaboration, slow progress, and low productivity.

LOW TRUST, RESPECT, AND RAPPORT

Without trust, respect, and rapport, team members don't like to seek coaching or mentoring from their leader. Coaching sessions don't produce the desired outcomes because team members don't show willingness to share personal information or discuss sensitive issues.

Team members often don't try to apply what they have learned in coaching sessions due to low buy-in and commitment to achieving results. Let me quote a study by the Journal of Occupational Health Psychology that reveals that employees who reported lower trust and respect for their supervisor also reported lower participation in coaching and mentoring activities.

Trust, respect, and rapport are necessary for team members to share personal or sensitive issues with their leader. In their absence, poor communication, low engagement, limited flexibility, ineffective problem-solving, lack of accountability, and weak relationships are some outcomes.

WHICH ONE IS MORE IMPORTANT FOR YOU AS A LEADER?

It is difficult to determine which one of trust, respect, and rapport is the most critical priority for a coaching conversation between a leader and their direct report, as all three are crucial elements of effective coaching.

Trust is vital because it allows your team members to feel safe and comfortable sharing personal stuff and discussing delicate issues with you. Trust is necessary for team members to open up and be candid in their coaching conversations. Respect is important because it allows team members to feel valued and appreciated. Team members feel less engaged and invested in the coaching process without respect. Rapport is crucial because it allows team members to build positive and effective relationships with you. Team members struggle to collaborate and work effectively with you if they don't feel a sense of connection with you.

 Research supports that trust, respect, and rapport are critical elements of effective coaching.

As a leader, you must practice listening actively to understand the team's perspectives and needs to increase trust, respect, and rapport in a coaching conversation. This can be achieved by:

1. Creating a safe, relaxed environment where team members feel comfortable sharing their thoughts, ideas, and concerns.
2. Showing a genuine interest in helping team members grow and develop professionally and personally.
3. Communicating with your team members consistently and transparently. Recognizing and rewarding good work can help build trust, respect, and rapport with team members.
4. Being steady in your actions, words, and follow-through will help build trust and respect with your team members.

5. Displaying empathy and understanding when team members go through difficult times can help establish trust and build rapport.
6. Showing openness to new ideas and perspectives can help build trust and respect with team members.
7. Providing constructive feedback can help team members improve their performance and build trust and rapport.

Building trust, respect, and rapport is an ongoing process; it takes time to establish it. To be more coach-like, leaders need to demonstrate these behaviors consistently.

Organizations that I help build coaching culture report that trust, respect, and rapport are essential factors in the coaching relationship between a leader and their Coachee. When these elements are present, team members feel comfortable and safe discussing highly private and personal issues with their leader in their coaching conversations, feel valued and respected, and have a positive and productive relationship.

 Together, leader-coach and their teams create an environment where teams can learn and grow, leading to better performance and productivity.

In the following chapters, let's learn the specific tools and strategies to build trust, respect, and rapport with your teams.

Pillar #1 – **Trust**

Speed-coaching conversations are deep and grounded in listening and understanding. That's why they create impact.

Think of one of the most powerful conversations that positively impacted your life. A dialogue that guided you in a different direction and opened up greater possibilities. A conversation that you believe that without having it, you would not have been where you are today.

Now, reflecting on that conversation, remember what was so special about that interaction? I have asked this question to thousands of participants in my training. The answers are something like this:

1. I sincerely trusted the person I was having this conversation with.
2. The person made me feel comfortable.
3. We both were deeply connected at a significantly more profound level.
4. The person took an interest in my well-being.
5. The person believed in me.
6. I didn't feel judged throughout the conversation.
7. The person didn't thrust their own opinion or advice on me.
8. The person was warm, encouraging, and motivating.
9. I left the conversation feeling better than when I entered the conversation.
10. The person listened to me without labelling my feelings or thoughts.

This type of conversation can only occur when the team trusts the leader, and their relationship is based on trust, not fear. On the contrary, when leaders exude fear, people feel a disconnect.

Let me ask you a power question. *'If I meet your team today and ask whether their relationship with you is trust-based or fear-based, what do you think their response be?'*

I keep asking this question before running Executive Coaching assignments with senior leaders or teaching a group of leaders the art of speed-coaching. I find very few leaders in a trust-based relationship with their team. Mostly, leaders admitted that it was based on threats, fears, and disrespect.

Trust is necessary for coaching. No coaching conversation can produce the desired outcomes if two people involved in the exchange don't trust each other, have no mutual respect, or don't feel some level of rapport and connection during the conversation.

Trust is critical for a coach-like leader to coach someone on their team effectively. We have witnessed groups that trust their leader easily open up, show vulnerability, and share their thoughts and feelings. This level of openness and vulnerability multiplies the impact of coaching.

Leaders can earn the trust of their teams by being transparent and consistent in their actions and decisions. Leaders can drastically increase mutual trust by effectively communicating and listening to team members, showing integrity and ethical behavior, taking responsibility for their mistakes, and providing support and resources for team members to succeed.

REWARDS OF TRUST

 As a coach-leader, you can build trust by treating team members respectfully and fairly and creating a positive and inclusive work environment. When you establish trust with the team and create a safe environment, the team feels comfortable sharing their deepest thoughts, feelings, and ideas.

Trust enables open and honest communication, which is crucial for effective coaching. When you establish trust as a leader, team members reveal their uncensored thoughts, allowing you to understand their perspectives better and help them achieve their goals. Trust also encourages the team to take risks and try new things.

Trust allows constructive feedback without fear of judgment. When trust is established, team members feel open to feedback, helping them grow and develop.

INGREDIENTS OF TRUST

When do you start trusting someone in a relationship? I have been asking this questions for years in my Speed Coaching training sessions. The answers are something like this:

You trust someone when you see them as reliable, capable, and truthful. Trust can also refer to reliance on a person or the feeling that someone or something will act in a certain way. Trust is a fundamental component of healthy relationships, allowing individuals to depend on and rely on one another.

Through our research with coach-like leaders, we have identified six key ingredients necessary for trust to develop and maintain between the coaching leader and their Coachees.

1. Honesty: Trust is built on transparency and openness. If a leader is consistently dishonest, it will be impossible for trust to develop.
2. Consistency: Trust is strengthened by dependable and consistent behavior. When leaders' actions align with their words, trust grows automatically.
3. Communication: Clear and open communication is essential for building trust and allows individuals to understand each other's needs, feelings, and perspectives.
4. Vulnerability: Trust requires vulnerability on both sides. Trust can grow stronger when leaders and followers are willing to share their thoughts, feelings, and fears.
5. Respect: Trust is built on mutual respect. Trust can develop when the leader and team respect each other's boundaries, opinions, and feelings.
6. Empathy: Readiness to put yourself in others' situation and feel for them builds instant bond. Trust dramatically increases when leaders empathize with their teams

TRUST SIGNS

 How would you know your team trusts you? What indicators show that you and your Coachees enjoy a reasonable degree of mutual trust? In my decade-long research, I have identified some essential elements:

When teams trust the leader, they support and implement the decision they co-take with the leader.

Knowing the leader has their best interests, they can take up any challenge.

Trusting relationships between leaders and team members lead to higher performance and productivity.

> **A team's trust in its leader positively impacts morale and motivation**

When coaching leaders earn the trust of their teams, members hold themselves accountable for their actions and progress, which helps produce better results from coaching conversations.

RESEARCH ON TRUST AND COACHING

Trust multiplies the effectiveness of coaching conversations promoting the development and growth of team members. Journal of Business and Technical Communication found that a team that trusts its leader is more open to feedback and coaching.

I found a similar study in Journal of Applied Psychology. It proves that employees who trust their leader are more satisfied with their job and more engaged and committed to the organization. In addition, a study by the Corporate Executive Board (CEB) reveals a strong correlation between trust and team productivity.

 Research also suggests that trust can help to create openness, better understanding, and greater willingness to take risks, increased buy-in, greater accountability, and more efficient conversations. In my follow-up training programs with participants of my 'Speed-Coaching' (Coaching Skills for Leaders Program), organizations repeatedly report that enhanced trust between their leaders and teams positively impacted coaching conversations and fostered a more productive and effective coaching relationship.

Another research in Journal of Applied Psychology discovered that employees who trust their leader are more engaged and committed to the organization, leading to higher productivity and performance. Journal of Management presents similar results revealing that trust in leaders is positively associated with team performance.

In our work with several organizations, we have also observed that trust leads to higher innovation and creativity. Reason is simple; teams feel more comfortable sharing their ideas and taking risks when they trust their leader. Over the years, my team and I have witnessed that mutual trust between a leader and their team positively impacts team's confidence and leads to more engaged, committed, and productive employees, ultimately driving the organization's success.

WHAT IF THERE IS A TRUST DEFICIT?

 Rebuilding broken trust can be challenging. However, there are scientifically proven methods to help build trust. Here are a few strategies:

Strategy #1:
Openness and honesty in communication are among the most critical factors in building trust. Coaching-leaders should be transparent about their intentions, actions, and decisions and actively listen to and address the concerns of their team members. Research published in the Journal of Applied Psychology found that transparent communication is positively associated with trust in leaders. Journal of Management found that leaders who communicate transparently are more trusted by their employees.

Strategy #2:
Experienced coach-leaders create opportunities for team members to work together on projects and initiatives, allowing them to get to know each other better and build trust. Journal of Applied Psychology's study found that team members with more interaction opportunities are likelier to trust one another.

Strategy #3:
Coach-Like leaders foster the habit of giving and receiving feedback and ensuring that feedback is constructive and respectful. This can help team members develop greater understanding and trust each other. To rebuild trust, leaders must encourage psychological safety in the team by supporting open and honest communication, valuing diversity, and fostering a positive and supportive work environment.

Psychological safety, defined as the belief that one will not be punished or humiliated for speaking up with ideas, questions, concerns, or mistakes, is positively related to trust in leaders. (**Journal of Applied Psychology**)

Strategy #4:

Holding your team members accountable for their actions and ensuring they take responsibility for their mistakes. This helps build trust by showing that everyone is held to the same standards and that the team is committed to achieving its goals. Accountability positively relates to trust in leaders. (Journal of Applied Psychology)

Invest in leadership development to ensure leaders have the skills and knowledge to build trust with their team members. Recognize and reward team members who exhibit trustworthy behavior, and this will encourage others to follow their example.

Strategy #5:

Creating a positive and productive environment where team members can communicate effectively, engage fully, take risks, solve problems, be accountable, and build strong relationships with their leader.

SHARED EXPERIENCES AND INTERACTIONS BUILD TRUST

 More than any strategies and tools, as a leader, you must practice what you preach and model the behavior you expect from your team. As a coaching leader, when you choose to be honest, keep promises, and be consistent in your actions, you will earn your team's trust and skyrocket the impact of your coaching conversations.

Pillar #2 – **Respect**

Our decade-long research revealed that people who do not respect their leader take coaching less seriously and are not much receptive to feedback. They feel discomfort discussing their performance with the leader, making it difficult for the leader to conduct effective coaching conversations and improve team's performance.

Someone asked the son of a tribal chief, *'how did you learn to be a great leader?'*

He responded that with his father in tribal meetings, he saw his father practicing two rituals in his interactions with older tribal fellows. The first thing was the sitting arrangements, and they always sat in circles. Secondly, he observed that his father was always the last person to speak.

This secret formula of ruling the hearts and minds is derived from the story of Nelson Mandela, one of the most respected leaders of our times.

Coach-like leaders understand the power of giving and gaining respect. They also know this rarely understood truth that one surest key unlocks the doorway to respect, and that is *'listening.'*

People respect you more when you speak less and listen to them more, when you seek more and show greater understanding. Offering people to share their opinions makes them feel respected. And in return, they respect you more. Additionally, you get to hear diverse approaches and improve your stance on the issue in question.

To coach effectively, earning respect is a must for the leader. A leader respected by the team is seen as credible and trustworthy, which is essential for building a solid coaching relationship.

EARN MORE RESPECT

A coaching leader who has earned respect can more easily address conflicts or issues within the team. Earning respect is critical in building an organization's thriving coaching culture. Here are a few ideas for leaders to gain more respect:

1. Demonstrating solid and practical leadership, making difficult decisions, being a good communicator, and providing clear guidance and direction for the team.
2. Listening carefully, being open to feedback and input from team members, and being willing to make adjustments based on their perspectives.

3. Being accountable for your actions means taking responsibility for your mistakes and being willing to admit when you are wrong.
4. Treating team members with respect, valuing their contributions, and treating them with dignity and fairness.
5. Leading by example sets a positive standard for professionalism, reliability, and ethics.
6. Being transparent and consistent in communication and following through on commitments.
7. Showing empathy, understanding team members' perspectives, and being flexible and adaptable to changing situations.

As a leader, you cannot demand respect. You must *earn respect* through consistent and positive actions. The fact is, respect is never given; it's consistently earned.

NO RESPECT, NO COACHING

When teams don't respect their leaders, it can lead to several negative consequences. Team productivity decreases as members are unwilling to follow instructions or take direction from someone they don't respect.

Teams don't feel invested in the organization's success, leading to high turnover rates and difficulty achieving goals. A lack of respect for leadership can lead to a toxic work environment and negatively impact the team's overall performance.

WHY RESPECT?

Our research with over 400 clients reveals that respect is essential for leaders to coach their teams because it establishes trust and credibility with team members. When team members respect their leader, they listen to feedback and be open to constructive criticism. They also feel comfortable approaching their leader with questions and concerns, resulting in better communication and problem-solving.

> When team members respect their leader, they go the extra mile to complete their job. Respect also allows leaders to create a positive work environment. Teams that respect their leaders will be more motivated and engaged, which can lead to higher job satisfaction and lower turnover rates.

Graduates of our 'Certified Coach-Like Leader' program report that respect is crucial to successful coaching because it helps leaders gain buy-in, cooperation, and commitment from their teams.

HOW CAN LEADERS EARN THE RESPECT OF THEIR TEAMS?

Respect and coaching effectiveness go hand in hand. When team members respect their leader, they are more likely to be receptive to coaching and open to feedback. There is no shortcut to earning respect from the team. Leaders can do quite a few things to earn respect from their teams:

1. Clear and consistent communication is essential for building trust and respect. Coaching-Leaders take the time to listen to their team members and respond to their questions and concerns.
2. Coaching-Leaders are open to feedback and willing to adapt to changing circumstances. This shows that they are eager to learn and grow as leaders.
3. Coaching-Leaders treat all team members with fairness and consistency. They are transparent in their decision-making and hold themselves accountable for their actions.
4. Coaching-Leaders lead by example and demonstrate the behavior and attitudes they expect from their team members.
5. Coaching-Leaders respect the team members' opinions, ideas, and contributions. They treat them with dignity and respect.

Also, recognizing and rewarding team members for their hard work and contributions can help build respect and loyalty.

HOW TO REGAIN RESPECT?

Leaders who earn the respect of their teams can create breakthroughs in coaching conversations. Their teams are more engaged and motivated, leading to better performance and positively impacting their productivity and overall success. We have observed that a respected leader has a better chance of conducting effective coaching conversations and improving the team's performance. ***Interestingly, a good coaching session helps build respect and trust between the leader and team members.***

Re-gaining respect can be challenging for coaching leaders, but it is possible. We have been proposing lots of effective strategies to leaders in multiple organizations to re-gain respect, and I am sharing the top five here with the highest success rate:

1. Follow through on commitments and decisions, be fair and consistent, and hold yourself accountable for your efforts.
2. Acknowledge any mistakes or poor decisions that may have led to a loss of respect and take responsibility for them.
3. Treat team members with dignity, and value their opinions, ideas, and contributions.
4. Recognize and reward team members for their hard work and contributions.
5. Continuously improve your leadership skills, and be able to inspire, motivate, coach, mentor, and develop your team members.

SCIENTIFIC EVIDENCE

Studies have shown that when team members respect their leader, they are more receptive to coaching and open to feedback. This creates a positive environment for coaching conversations, where team members feel comfortable discussing their performance and goals and working together to improve.

 A research in the Journal of Occupational Health Psychology confirms that employees who felt respected by their supervisors reported higher levels of job satisfaction, organizational commitment, and well-being than those who did not feel respected.

Research has also shown that respect is a crucial ingredient in successful coaching. When team members respect their leader, they are more receptive to coaching and open to feedback.

MORE RESPECT, MORE IMPACTFUL COACHING

Several examples and case studies demonstrate the impact of a leader's enhanced respect on coaching their teams. In a case study published in the Harvard Business Review, a CEO of a manufacturing company was able to turn around the performance by earning the respect of his employees through open and transparent communication, a willingness to listen to their concerns, and a focus on building trust and respect. As a result, the employees were more willing to accept feedback and coaching, which led to improved performance and a more engaged workforce.

 A study from the Journal of Occupational Health Psychology discovered that a leader's respect for their employees was positively associated with employees' perceptions of their leader's ability to provide effective coaching and feedback. The researchers found that when employees felt respected by their leader, they responded positively to the coaching process, which led to improved performance and well-being.

International Journal of Human Resource Management published a research describing how a team's respect for their leader led to improved coaching conversations, better performance, and employee engagement. The leader in this case study actively listened to employee concerns, provided regular feedback, and recognized and rewarded employee contributions. As a result, employees felt respected and valued, which led to improved performance, better communication, and a more engaged workforce.

These examples demonstrate how enhanced respect between leader and team can positively impact coaching outcomes and overall culture.

RESPECT IS CRITICAL FOR COACHING

The University of Colorado found that employees who feel respected by their leaders are more likely to respond positively to feedback and coaching, leading to improved performance. Leading by example and modeling the behavior and attitudes that you expect from your team members can help you gain respect from your team.

A recent research published in the Journal of Occupational Health Psychology found that employees who perceive their leaders as consistent and fair in their actions and decisions report higher levels of respect for their leaders. Being consistent in your actions, decision-making, and following through on commitments can help you gain respect from your team.

International Journal of Human Resource Management published that leaders who continuously improve their leadership skills, inspire, motivate, coach, mentor, and develop their team members are more likely to be respected by their team members.

RESPECT BASED CONVERSATIONS

Studies and data suggest that respect is crucial in productive coaching conversations. An influential study from the Journal of Occupational Health Psychology revealed that a leader's respect for their employees was positively associated with employees' perceptions of their leader's ability to provide effective coaching and feedback. The study found that when employees felt respected by their leader, they responded more positively to feedback and coaching, which led to improved performance and well-being.

Our observation confirms that showing appreciation and recognition for the team's hard work and contributions helps leaders gain respect and have more productive coaching conversations.

PSYCHOLOGICAL TOOLS FOR GAINING RESPECT

Our research with leaders who mastered the art of coaching conversations reveals the secret psychological tool they use to multiply respect and impact in coaching. I am sharing some of those psychology-based tools along with their scientific evidence.

1. Active Listening:
    To me, listening is the doorway to respect. Research in the Journal of Occupational Health Psychology found that active listening positively correlates with employees' perceptions of their leader's ability to provide effective coaching and feedback. The study proves that when leaders actively listen to employee concerns, employees feel respected and valued, which leads to improved performance and well-being.

2. Empathy:
    Empathy allows coaching leaders to enter into their Coachee's world. Journal of Applied Psychology explains that employees feel more positively towards their leaders and the organization when they show empathy. Psychologists found that empathy and compassion can help leaders create a positive and respectful coaching environment.

3. Positive reinforcement:
    All behaviors are driven by reinforcements. Journal of Organizational Behavior revealed that positive reinforcement is positively associated with powerful coaching dialogues, improved employee performance, and well-being.

4. Feedback:

   Two-way feedback is the motorway of superior performance and healthy relationships between leaders and teams. A Journal of Applied Psychology study found that feedback positively correlates with improved employee performance. The researchers discovered that when leaders provide feedback respectfully and constructively, employees feel more respected and valued, which leads to improved performance.

5. Transparent communication:

   I learned a power phrase many years back, which changed my perception of leadership. It says, 'Quality of your leadership is the quality of your communication'. Journal of Management found that transparent communication positively correlates with improved employee trust and respect for their leaders.

6. Self-awareness:

   Coaching is about raising the self-awareness of the person you coach instead of telling them what you think they should be doing. Journal of Applied Psychology discovered that self-awareness positively correlates with improved leadership effectiveness. The study found that leaders who are self-aware are more likely to be influential leaders who can gain respect from their team members.

Many leaders in our coaching programs try bypassing the *'No respect, No coaching'* truth. They think they can do away without it. However, research proves the opposite.

I also teach leaders that earning respect is not an overnight endeavor. Leaders must consistently demonstrate respect to the teams and use various psychological tools to gain respect. At the same time, leaders must understand that gaining respect is more about living with the mindset of 'mutual respect' rather than using techniques to look for ways to *expect and demand* respect.

 Much psychological research and data support using psychological tools such as active listening, empathy, positive reinforcement, feedback, transparent communication, reflective feedback, and self-awareness to earn the team's respect while coaching them.

When you adopt a mindset that believes in giving and *earning* respect, these tools can provide additional support to create a positive and respectful coaching environment, leading to improved coaching conversations, enhanced performance, and maximized productivity for the leader, team and organization.

Pillar #3 – **Rapport**

No rapport, no coaching conversation. Period.

How many people on your team make you act natural and allow you to be yourself in their presence? These are the people you in rapport with.

When we are around people we feel a rapport with, we experience a sense of warmth, connection, and comfort. Deep down inside, we share a moment of relatedness with those people. We experience it briefly or over a more extended period of interaction with someone. It can happen in transitory interactions or expressed as *'It's always a delight being with you.'* Rapport is at the essence of every coaching relationship. In a way, rapport is the quality of coaching connections.

> As a coach-like leader, your job is to build comfort and confidence for your team members. Your leadership style should challenge them and encourage them to think for themselves rather than give them solutions. Sometimes, you must give them critical feedback that is hard to digest. To do this, you and your team must enjoy a deep rapport.

When leaders build rapport with their teams, they influence them constructively without pressuring, telling, or dictating through coaching conversations.

Rapport brings you and your Coachee on the same page. You feel a sense of sameness and share a similar mental model about things, situations, and events. As a coach-leader, you will discover that rapport is not static and can go up or down during a coaching conversation. Therefore, the connection you experience with your Coachee does affect the feelings and behavior of both of you.

Rapport provides the foundation for a coaching conversation. When you and your Coachee feel comfortable with each other, you both act more openly and share more authentically. Rapport removes unnecessary masks and encourages an atmosphere where coaches and Coachee feel comfortable being themselves. When you consciously build rapport, you fill coaching interaction and the work environment with comfort, creativity, and connection.

What do you think is the opposite of rapport?

It is detachment or disconnect. People don't open up without rapport and fail to build trust.

NO RAPPORT EXERCISE

Think for a moment about someone you don't have a rapport with and answer the following questions:

1. Do you feel natural in their presence?
2. Can you be yourself while you are with them?
3. What does your mind tell you about this person?
4. Does it signal your differences, or does the focus go to similarities?

Here are some of those feelings participants in my training share about not being in rapport with someone in a meeting or interaction:

- The other person didn't show warmth.
- I felt less comfortable and natural in the conversation and
- The quality of mutual understanding was way below.
- I felt a sense of separation, detachment, and difference towards the person.
- I felt less able to express myself.

EXPERIENCING RAPPORT

On the contrary, think of someone you feel a complete rapport with and answer the below questions:

1. What is your feeling when you are in their company?
2. Do you focus on similarities or differences?
3. Have you noticed the impact of your rapport with this person on your behavior, thoughts, and feelings?
4. How is this experience different from being with someone with whom your connection is missing?

Your ability to think for the other person you coach drastically impacts the rapport and coaching dialogue. When you can put yourself in their shoes and feel what they feel, you automatically build a sense of relatedness with your team, allowing you to say or do things that make them feel comfortable with you.

Empathy can provide you with the foundation to build rapport with your team. A sense of connection increases your ability to influence your team and get them to take on greater ownership of their actions without you telling, monitoring, or dictating them.

> As a Leadership Coach for the past twenty years, I have experienced rapport building as one of the most rewarding skills. It fills my heart with great satisfaction when I see a visible shift in people's response within a few minutes of our interaction.

When I coach executives, they initially sit with preconceived notions and judgments and sometimes with a *'know it all'* mindset. Novice coaches might find it very intimidating. However, this skepticism is not bothersome at all. Beyond a shadow of a doubt, my conviction keeps telling me that I am going to build another lifelong, trust-based relationship with this person.

Establishing rapport is an essential aspect of effective coaching for a coach-like leader. When leaders connect with their team, they create a sense of trust and understanding that forms the foundation of a strong coaching relationship. Building rapport allows leaders to understand better their Coachees' perspectives, needs, and goals.

In our coaching demos during the training sessions, we notice that Coachees become open and honest when a leader develops rapport, allowing for more effective feedback. Establishing rapport also allows the leader to identify areas of strength and improvement for each team member, which can help them construct more result-oriented coaching conversations.

Building rapport helps leaders create a more positive and supportive environment. Team members feel more comfortable approaching the leader with concerns or ideas and taking the leader's feedback on board, becoming more productive and engaged.

HOW DO COACH-LEADERS BUILD RAPPORT?

In my training programs, I conduct a simple exercise. I ask a volunteer to sit on the stage and act as a leader who doesn't enjoy a great rapport with their team. I encourage other participants to give suggestions, ideas, and advice on how to build rapport with their team. The list goes something like this:

1. Become a good listener
2. Communicate expectations, goals, and feedback
3. Be transparent and consistent
4. Follow through on commitments
5. Show empathy and understanding
6. Be aware of the perspectives and needs of team members
7. Make an effort to understand their points of view
8. Be approachable and open to feedback
9. Be available to team members
10. Reassure them to share their ideas and concerns
11. Create a positive work environment
12. Foster a culture of respect, collaboration, and inclusivity
13. Recognize and reward good work
14. Be a good role model and lead by example

As a coaching leader, you must understand that establishing rapport with your team requires consistent effort. Being approachable, understanding, and trustworthy will help your team feel more comfortable and willing to share their ideas and perspectives with you in coaching conversations.

PSYCHOLOGICAL TOOLS TO BUILD RAPPORT

As an organizational psychologist, I fully utilize psychological tools to build rapport. Over the years, I have shared many tried and tested methods to make an instant rapport and connection, and I am sharing a few of them here:

1. Active listening:
   Listen actively and attentively to the person you are coaching and show that you are engaged by nodding, making eye contact, and responding to what they say. Beyond an informal coaching conversation, a coaching leader pays complete attention to the team with real presence and consistent eye contact with every room member.

2. Reflective language:

   Use reflective language to repeat or paraphrase what the Coachee says, showing that you understand their perspective and are on the same wavelength.

3. Empathy:

   Show empathy by understanding the Coachee's feelings and acknowledging their perspective, which can help to build trust and mutual understanding.

4. Open-ended questions:

   Use open-ended questions to encourage the Coachee to share their thoughts and feelings, which can help to establish a deeper connection and understanding.

5. Matching and mirroring:

   Match and mirror the Coachee's body language, tone of voice, and pace of speech, which can help to establish rapport and show that you are on the same page. Richard Bandler and John Grinder proposed Matching & mirroring techniques extensively used in Neuro-Linguistic Programming.

 Pacing and leading are two additional techniques to navigate the rapport once developed by matching the energy and mirroring the feeling of understanding and acknowledgment. This spark of connection, coupled with power questions, leads the Coachee toward greater self-awareness and responsibility.

After 35 years of studying human behavior, Milton Erickson (a medical doctor, Psychologist, and hypnotherapist) discovered that when people meet people, they mirror each other. The energy, vibes, and feelings are reciprocal. He further explains that coaching leaders must use this to establish a real, authentic, and genuine connection.

RAPPORT KILLERS

Through my observation and research, I have identified numerous habits and behaviors that can decrease rapport during a coaching conversation. Here is my top list of such behaviors and their impact on the Coachee. It would be best if you avoided them to stay in rapport.

1. Interrupting or talking over the person can make them feel unheard and disrespected.
2. Being judgmental or critical can make the person feel defensive and unwilling to share their thoughts and feelings.
3. Not understanding the person's perspective and not acknowledging their feelings can make them feel unsupported and unimportant.
4. Not being transparent, honest, and consistent can decrease trust and mutual understanding.
5. Being too directive or giving too much advice can make the person feel like they need to be heard and respected and can decrease their motivation for learning and growth.
6. Not listening actively and attentively to the person you are coaching can make them feel unimportant and disengaged. The inability to communicate effectively can lead to misunderstanding and decrease rapport.
7. Being dismissive or unresponsive can make the person feel unimportant and disengaged.

LEVEL OF RAPPORT

Rapport is never constant and keeps moving from one level to the other. It's important to note that the level of rapport can vary depending on the coaching conversation, the topic, and the people involved. Coach-like leaders can experience three levels of rapport in their day-to-day interactions with their teams, including coaching conversations.

1. Surface level rapport:
   This is the initial level of connection, where the leader-coach and team members get to know each other and build a basic level of trust and understanding. Surface-level rapport is often established through small talk and casual conversation before a coaching conversation.

2. Intermediate level rapport:
   A deeper understanding and trust between the leader and team members characterizes this rapport. At this level, the coach-leader and team members may share more personal information and begin to build a deeper level of connection.

3. Deep-level rapport:
   This is the highest level of rapport, where the coaching leader and team members feel a strong connection and understanding. At this level, they enjoy the deeper trust and mutual respect and can have open and honest coaching conversations, even on sensitive topics.

The rapport levels during a coaching conversation can differ depending on the topic or situation. For example, the rapport can be more profound when discussing a personal development plan than a performance issue.

REBUILDING RAPPORT

Rapport is not constant. Sometimes, during the coaching conversation, leaders lose a sense of rapport. If you see a disconnection with your team, here's how you can rebuild rapport as a coach-like leader.

1. Acknowledge the disconnection: Be honest, acknowledge a disconnection, and express your willingness to work on rebuilding the relationship.
2. Apologize if necessary: If you realize you have made a mistake, apologize and take responsibility for your actions.
3. Re-establish trust: Be transparent, honest, and reliable, and make a conscious effort to follow through on your commitments.
4. Listen carefully: Take the time to listen to your team members and understand their perspectives, feelings, and concerns. Show that you are engaged by nodding, making eye contact, and responding to what they say.
5. Take time for conversations: Make time for one-on-one discussions with team members to build deeper connections and understanding.
6. Use open-ended questions: Use open-ended questions more frequently to encourage the person you coach to share their thoughts and feelings. This will help establish a deeper connection and understanding.
7. Validate their feelings: Show appreciation and validate the person's feelings and thoughts, which can help them feel heard and understood.

Leader and Coachee, at times, can be in two different worlds. Hence, the rapport can disconnect. Re-establishing a connection when the coach and the Coachee have different perspectives can be challenging.

It will be helpful if you invest time in identifying the cause of the disconnection and understand the reasons, whether it is a lack of communication, understanding, or a difference in perspective. As a coach-leader, try to understand the other person's context. Try knowing where they come from, what they care about, and what they struggle with.

Research by Mathew et al. 2008, indicates that ***we like people who are either like us or like how we would like to be in the future***. If they fail to meet these criteria, we often try to ignore the possibility of finding a connection. Two additional, most foundational steps towards building rapport as a coaching leader are:

1. Undivided attention
2. Positive verbal and non-verbal communication

As a coach-leader, always remember that every team member needs a total response during each interaction with you while speaking, sharing, or discussing their assignment, opinion, or feedback. Coach-like leaders allow team members to experience the feeling of being "heard" and "understood" and make them feel important.

 ACTIONS

1. During a coaching conversation, build appropriate levels of rapport to help the Coachees feel comfortable and to encourage natural conversation.
2. Create a suitable climate and warmth for the conversation.
3. Make your Coachee feel that they are in safe hands.

Stage 04

PRACTICE
Speed Coaching as a Way of Life

Chapter #9 – Transitioning from Bossing to Coaching
- From task to connection
- From crisis to calmness
- From deadline to growth

Chapter #10 – Overcoming Speed Coaching Barriers
- Resistance
- Importance
- Preference

Chapter 09

★ **The Transition from Bossing to Coaching**

The Transition from Bossing to Coaching

Transition is never comforting. Human beings fear change, and we resist trying something new. We build imaginary mountains of negative consequences convincing us that transition will be impossible. Sometimes we fear transition so severely that we do not even talk about adverse outcomes, let alone be willing to experience one. However, the only thing we resist is our growth and the opportunity to experience a higher level of living.

To help leaders transition from being a boss to becoming more *coach-like*, I have been conducting research with global leaders to discover their preferred leadership. My team and I have also been enabling leaders to distinguish a boss-like leader from a coach-like one.

> Boss-like leaders give directions with a top-down management style. Followers and their needs are not the primary concern in boss-like leadership. Instead, an aggressive leadership style ensures maximum output with the least possible investment.

These long-standing leadership practices have served managers for decades with a greater return in the areas such as clarity in the chain of command and consistent results. However, in the 21st century, teams strongly resist boss-like leadership, demanding a more humanistic leadership style.

In contrast, coach-like leaders put employees and their needs as the paramount concern of their leadership focus. Coaching contends with traditional leadership and urges leaders to see teams as a whole and not limited to their designations, roles, and tasks.

Coaching leaders take extra pain to peep into their teams' emotional and psychological worlds, catering to the most fundamental needs on which human motivation resides. Therefore, the coach-like leaders act as captains of the ship and feel responsible for every crew member's life, security, and safe return home.

OBSTACLES TO COACHING

According to our research, several obstacles can prevent team leaders from effectively coaching their team members, including:

1. Managers lack the necessary knowledge or *training in coaching* techniques and principles. Training is often either ineffective or irrelevant to workplace challenges and may be misaligned entirely with environmental realities.
2. They find it difficult to *relinquish control* and empower team members. This is the toughest one. When managers think they will lose their sense of power and control over people, they resist the transition.
3. They somehow *prioritize task-oriented goals* over employee development. Managers these days conveniently outsource the developmental part to the HR department and keep their focus on getting the results through their teams.
4. Managers face *trouble in providing constructive feedback* sensitively and effectively. Giving feedback is an art that most people are unskilled in.

5. *Fear of appearing weak* or less competent. Giving answers allows managers to feel in control and prove their competence. Therefore, their resistance to coach prevails.

6. They have *limited time* and resources to devote to coaching activities. However, speed coaching is totally the opposite. Instead of making time for it, managers utilize daily interactions to create a coaching experience.

7. Managers *lack the basic trust and rapport* with team members required for coaching. Therefore, the command and control style takes priority.

THE TRANSITION

Based on our research, we have identified three specific distinctions between the two styles. Our observation is that once leaders understand the difference, they show more receptiveness to transition from bossing to a coaching style.

Transition #1: **FROM TASK TO CONNECTION**

A boss-like leader seems to care more about completing the task than building rapport and connection. They don't ask their team members about their task challenges. As a result, the team often delivers the job without creativity and a personal touch.

 On the other hand, Coach-like leaders appear to be invested in building deep relationships with their teams. They offer their full support and encouragement with a proactive presence in words and actions. The coaching leadership style is hard to develop but very convenient to run as a natural process to bring out the best in people. We have witnessed teams working with a coach-like leader experiment more in the face of a challenging goal and show readiness to go beyond the call of duty to match their leaders' trust in their competence and capabilities.

Consequently, the results significantly improve with enhanced determination and personal responsibility. Teams give their blood and sweat and feel a more profound sense of ownership.

Transition #2: **FROM CRISIS TO CALM**

 Boss-like leaders must build a composed behavior in times of crisis or emergency, especially in the post-Covid 19 world. Since the boss-like leader leads in isolation, difficult times make him suffer the most. In frustration and haste to control the uncontrollable, the boss worsens the situation by losing the trust and confidence of his team.

Coach-like leader, on the other hand, manages crisis gracefully with the help of his team, following the "we are all in this together "approach. A problem is when a coach-like leader demonstrates his maximum influence and impact by keeping the team collected under one mission and constantly inspiring them to continue working with more resilience and perseverance.

Coach-leader has won the team's hearts, and he connects with his employees. Their team believes in their vision beyond the temporary situation. Subsequently, the group displays solidarity and support beyond their assigned roles and monetary rewards, resulting in a far more competitive team than any other.

Transition #3: **FROM DEADLINE TO GROWTH**

Last but not least is the area of focus where these two leadership styles highlight vital differences. The boss-like leader focuses on the deadlines with a *"here and now"* tone. However, the coach-like leader focuses on the long-term goals achieved by empowered and responsible employees.

A coach-like leader gives more time for long-term benefit and keeps quality distinct from quantity.

Now, what is your preferred style? Bossing or Coaching?

WHY MAKE A TRANSITION?

After spending years helping leaders adopt a coaching style of leadership, I have found three core reasons that persuade managers to choose Coaching over bossing.

Reason #1: **MAXIMUM EMPLOYEE ENGAGEMENT**

"The best executive is the one who has sense enough to pick good men to do what he wants done and self-restraint to keep from meddling with them while they do it."– Theodore Roosevelt.

People management is not easy, and leadership roles are becoming more demanding. According to research by the International Coach Federation (ICF), companies with active coaching cultures report 8% more employee engagement than those with poor coaching cultures.

Coach-like leader achieves higher employee engagement with a few primary behavioral shifts. They works on the employees' strengths by improving his knowledge of employees' capabilities and talents. They identify the right person for the right task assigning a perfect blend of challenge and skill to accomplish the task with full engagement.

On the contrary, a boss-like leader has limited insight into the employees' potential and generally gets stuck on designation, performance record, and safe play mindset. They also require the foresight to challenge their under-performers with appropriate task allocation.

Resultantly, employees keep doing same type of work for years and years, with no excitement and minimum utilization of their potential.

Reason #2: **GREATER RESPONSIBILITY AND OWNERSHIP**

Coach-like leaders in value teams in the decision-making process. Coaching instills greater responsibility and ownership among team members and builds their self-confidence to improve their self-efficacy. Every team member is valuable in a coaching culture, refuting the hierarchical demarcation, control, and command regime.

Boss-like leaders are less effective here in developing a mechanism where employees are conscientious and able to self-regulate. Boss-like leaders exert much time in surveillance and keeping checks and balances to keep the team focused on the goals.

Thus, the boss-like leader shows more burnout than an average coach-like leader.

Reason #3: **OPENNESS TO LEARNING AND DEVELOPMENT**

 Coaching opens an exotic door of continuous learning and development for the team and the leader. Bossing is often about being the perfect or epitome of excellence and competence, somehow creating a superficial image of expertise. Genuine ability is an ongoing process of constant learning and development.

Instead of judging employees by their failures, when leaders coach them on their shortcomings, it develops an atmosphere of a growth mindset. People do not hide or hold back their weaknesses, showing more openness and willingness to improve and convert weaknesses into strengths. Where do you see yourself in terms of transitioning from bossing to coaching?

Overcoming Speed Coaching Barriers

Overcoming Speed Coaching Barriers

Every Speed Coaching intervention we orchestrate for a client has an inbuilt post-training follow-through stage. In between training and follow-up, participants spend 10-12 weeks applying coaching concepts at the workplace under the supervision of their designated, experienced coaches from my team.

In my last two decades of developing coach-like leaders, I have seen leaders resist practicing coaching in their daily interactions with their teams. When we dig deeper, we find one of the three key reasons. These reasons are used as an excuse to treat coaching as a *Rest in Peace* (RIP' phenomenon.

Here are the three critical barriers preventing leaders from practice coaching conversations at the workplace.

1. **R**esistance - I am not convinced about coaching
2. **I**mportance - I don't have time to coach
3. **P**reference - I am tempted to manage

Let's talk about each one of them in more detail.

Barrier #1

RESISTANCE

When asked to give their honest feelings, managers admit that they are not entirely convinced about coaching their direct reports. Most managers still use the *'do it my way'* approach rather than seeing their teams through the possibility lens.

SELF-ANALYSIS

I suggest that if you feel the same resistance, ask yourself the following questions:

1. Do I believe in my team, or am I being fogged by my biases?
2. How am I showing up today? Am I energetic, positive, and enthusiastic?
3. What am I projecting through my interactions with my team?
4. Am I demonstrating total commitment to my team's development through my daily interactions with them?

IMPORTANCE

If we give proper importance to something, it will find space in our daily schedules automatically. Many managers that we interact with don't put a higher priority on coaching their direct reports. therefore, they need help finding enough minutes to start a coaching conversation with their teams.

Here is my solution to all those who struggle to speed-coach and complain about not having sufficient time for coaching conversations. You need to install two fundamental beliefs in your mind about speed coaching:

Belief #1:
You don't have to conclude a coaching conversation in one interaction. Coaching can be an ongoing discussion. If you cannot finish the conversation in 4-5 minutes or whatever little time you had, reconnect with them in the next interaction and pick up from your last question.

Belief #2:
If approached when the situation does not allow for an in-depth conversation, leaving the Coachee with a powerful coaching question and an invitation to pick up the conversation later is entirely appropriate.

RESPONDING TO A COACHING SITUATION:

How do you respond to such situations when you are pressed with time but cannot leave the Coachee on their own and don't want to fix the problem by giving advice?

In his book 'Stealth Coaching,' Rob Kramer has suggested five beautiful ways to respond when a coaching conversation is impossible due to time shortage.

RESPONSE #1

"This sounds intriguing. I do not have time to discuss it now, as I have this report to complete. Let's look at the calendar and set up a time to talk at the earliest opportunity this afternoon. Will that work for you?"

RESPONSE #2

'I have to get to my next meeting. In the meantime, consider what might be causing this confusion between you and this person.

RESPONSE #3

'You appear stuck. Given how you have handled similar issues, what might you try this time? Think about that, and we can talk more over lunch.'

RESPONSE #4

If you were in my position, what would you say to me? Mull that over tonight. I have to get to my appointment, but I want to talk further. Please add a meeting to my calendar for tomorrow.'

RESPONSE #5

What might be at the root of it? And if you could have the interaction again, what would you do differently? Think about that, and let's pick it up when I get back from my meeting.'

Barrier #3

PREFERENCE

Managers and leaders have been so comfortable with traditional management practices that they find difficult adjusting to this new way of leading. Acting like a coaching leader takes serious effort. They sometimes try coaching quite half-heartedly and then embrace back their previously tried and tested tools like advising, commanding, and problem-fixing.

This temptation to manage becomes a habit.

In his book Coaching Habit, Michael Bungay Stanier beautifully explained this dilemma. He suggests that instead of the whole coaching process, you may start with one question at a time. Here are the seven powerful coaching questions Michael presented in his book.

1. What's on your mind?
2. And what else?
3. What's the real challenge here for you?
4. What do you want?
5. How can I help?
6. If you're saying yes to this, what are you saying no to?
7. What was most beneficial for you?

Even if you know nothing about coaching, asking one of these questions in response to a coaching situation (instead of advising) can open new doors of awareness and action for your direct reports. All you have to do is ask a question and then go silent and listen. You will figure out that coaching does work.

If you put aside your personal bias for your ideas and become open to listening to others' ideas, you will find it easy to transition from bossing to a coaching leadership style. The goal is to become more coach-like, not boss-like.

ASSESS YOURSELF

Coaching and bossing are two sides of the coin. Depending on the situation, you may choose one of these sides.

COMMAND & CONTROL MANAGER	COACH-LIKE LEADER
Reacts to **past mistakes**	Envisions **future potential** and aligns efforts around it
Pushes others to **overcome weaknesses**	Encourages people to **develop talents** and strengths
Steps to **solve others' problems**	**It helps people to identify, solve** and **prevent** problems
Sees managing as **"what I do."**	Sees managing as **"who I am."**

MANAGERS' EXCUSES FOR NOT SPEED COACHING

 In addition to the RIP barriers, over the years, my coaching supervisors and I have discovered nine frequently used excuses used by leaders around the globe for rejecting the idea of coaching.

Impactful Coaching Conversations

When managers ignore the application of the ATM Formula, here are some of the justifications they present to their coaching supervisors:

1. I couldn't spot the coaching opportunity. Sorry, I missed it.
2. My team needed an urgent solution. So, I didn't speed coach.
3. This problem required a quick answer; therefore, I didn't speed-coach.
4. When I start coaching, my team shuts down and doesn't respond to coaching questions.
5. My team needs to be more reliable in creating their solutions. So, I have to give them mine.
6. I am ready to coach, but my team needs to be prepared for coaching. They are used to getting solutions from me, and it will take time for them to adjust to my coaching style.
7. Coaching is a soft thing; my team is a bunch of hard nuts to crack, and coaching is not for them.
8. My team is not willing to get coached. They resist it.
9. I still need to improve at coaching, and I avoid it because I don't want to harm my team.
10. Coaching is not my cup of tea.

What is your excuse for not coaching your team?

PART 03

SPEED COACHING CULTURE

This part of the book takes you beyond a one-off coaching conversation and shares the process, barriers, solutions, and strategies of sowing the seeds of a coaching culture in the organization and nurturing it constantly to make coaching a way of life in your organization, family, and community.

Chapter 11

 Seeding a Speed Coaching Culture

Seeding a Speed Coaching Culture

Coaching is not just a technique. It is not a framework you use once in a while in a workplace conversation. Coaching, to me, is a way of life. Coaching is something to live and breathe in your interaction with other human beings.

There was a time when coaching aimed at derailing behaviors only, and managers took it as a tool to correct people and performance. Today coaching is widely used in organizations to develop high-potential employees, build future leaders, develop their strengths, and maximize their ability to have meaningful conversations with employees, peers, and even superiors.

How would you know whether your organization has a coaching culture or not?

ASK YOURSELF

1. Does your organization consider coaching as a serious leadership development tool?
2. Does your organization democratize coaching tools and frameworks so everyone utilizes coaching techniques in daily interactions?
3. Do leaders in your company prefer to embrace the coaching style of leadership as their favored way of leading?

WHAT MAKES A COACHING CULTURE?

You cannot build a coaching culture by hiring an external coach to run a coaching assignment with one or two of your key executives. A coaching culture is created when an organization crosses the boundaries of formal coaching and instills informal coaching as part of daily interactions.

In our work with several organizations worldwide, we have noticed that the organizations that build a coaching culture instill in their employees the mindset and skillset to embrace coaching. People fearlessly engage in conversations with each other, and these conversations are based on candidness and respect. Their reporting relationships don't obstacle these conversations. The focus is on improving the working relationship at an individual and collective level.

Organizations that embed coaching in their culture make a conscious effort to produce Coach-Like Leaders. These leaders can think like a coach, feel like a coach, listen like a coach, and talk like a coach. They understand the power of feedback and use feedback exchange as the most influential learning tool.

Coach-Like Leaders produce a high-trust relationship with the people around them. The strength of this relationship allows them to connect with people at a whole new level. People feel the inner drive to give their very best. Accept more challenging roles. Take greater responsibility for the results and continuously improve performance.

 Our research findings outline some of the most frequently witnessed features of a coaching culture:

1. Everyone in the organization speaks the common coaching language
2. Leaders role model the behaviors they want to instill in their teams
3. People at all levels show openness to feedback.
4. Coaching flows in all directions, up, down, and sideways.
5. Decisions are made and executed faster with complete ownership.

According to the Behavior Coaching Institute, a coaching culture guarantees reduced employee turnover, increased productivity, and greater employee happiness and satisfaction at work. Another research by Eldridge and Dmobowski reveals that a coaching culture promotes open communication, builds trust and respect, and improves working relationships.

 In a coaching culture, employees begin to recognize their role in facilitating the development of others. They take pride in enabling others to take charge of their growth and produce extraordinary results without being pushed, monitored, or supervised.

When organizations engage us to build a coaching culture, generally, this discussion starts with one fundamental question: *'Where is our next generation of leaders coming from?'*. Organizations committed to strengthening their leadership pipeline are eager to find creative and strategic ways of building a sustained leadership pipeline.

Coaching is the way of making this possible for them – faster. Because fostering a coaching culture eventually means the organization is committed to accelerating the development of its leaders and other high-potential employees.

Before building a coaching culture in your organization, you must focus on aligning coaching with your organization's strategic business goals. Without this alignment, coaching will fail to produce the desired impact.

Coaching should not be aimed at correcting performance; coaching is not meant for those who have already been written off or are at risk of being fired. We clarify to the organizations that a coaching culture cannot be created by viewing coaching as an intervention for poor performers.

FIVE ELEMENTS OF SEEDING A SPEED COACHING CULTURE

Based on our years of research and observation, here are the five critical steps you need to take to build a coaching culture in your organization.

Factor #1: **IDENTIFYING THE LEADERSHIP BEHAVIORS**

Have you fully articulated the leadership behaviors you want to reinforce as part of your coaching culture? Some of the top behaviors our clients want us to strengthen through coaching culture are the following:

1. Respectfully hold each other accountable for the behaviors and business results
2. Role model the behaviors leaders want to see across the organization
3. Demonstrate a greater sense of responsibility
4. Engage with people through an open exchange of dialog
5. Play an active role in the learning and development
6. Using two fundamental coaching tools in every interaction, i.e., asking powerful questions and deep listening.

Factor #2: **CLARIFY YOUR END GAME**

Does your partner (external coaching body or coaching firm) fully understand your organization's vision and strategy? Did they invest a significant amount of time knowing your company's culture?

You must ensure that the coaching is aligned with the strategy and vision and fully supports it. Coaching interventions should also reinforce the values of the organization. It is vital for the externally engaged coaching partners to know how your organization will measure and quantify the success of this initiative. It would be best if you clarified your expectations and the return on investment measure.

You should also deliberately align coaching culture with your 'people strategy.' If aligned well, the culture will focus on coaching through feedback, continuous learning, and accountability.

Factor #3: **ALIGN COACHING WITH YOUR LEADERSHIP FRAMEWORK**

Have you allied the coaching program with your leadership framework and other leadership development initiatives? Your internal and external coaches should invest time in understanding your leadership pipeline. This might include course outlines of different offerings, leadership competencies, and assessments used to spot and develop leaders.

Coaches need to know the skills and behaviors taught in those courses and see their relevance in building a coaching culture. Coaches can also plan to leverage business meetings, group interactions, forums for high potentials, and orientation sessions to leverage the reinforcement of core concepts of creating a coaching culture.

Factor #4: **CREATING A FEEDBACK LOOP**

Contrary to the traditional one-way command and control communication style, coaching conversations produce a meaningful, two-way feedback loop. When leaders act like coaches and build a proper feedback loop, it results in continuous learning and growth of their teams.

This feedback loop ensures that ideas are exchanged, the truth is heard, and responsibility is accepted, not imposed. The ultimate benefit of a coaching culture is that leaders start spotting coachable moments. Instead of telling people what they think they should do, they develop an eye for finding opportunities to coach their teams and exchange feedback.

Factor #5: BUILD A POWERFUL COACHING TEAM

Building a team of internal coaches with a shared mindset and passion for coaching is critical in building a coaching culture.

What is your process of selecting, training, and facilitating qualified coaches? How will you identify them, train them, equip them with coaching skills and processes, and evaluate their success? Building a team of coaches is not enough. You need to constantly keep these coaches informed and updated on the latest tools and trends of coaching.

> **A coaching culture is beyond using external coaches to run executive coaching assignments. Coaching culture lays the foundation of accepting coaching as a form of interacting with others, and a way of being.**

 In all the assignments we have accepted in the last two decades, we have always convinced the top leaders to role model the coaching behaviors themselves. It means coaching culture starts at the top. Once leaders at the top are convinced to walk the talk, they understand that coaching culture requires a strategic, comprehensive, and systemic approach to developing future leaders.

Coaching culture becomes a reality when leaders at the top level exhibit courage, engage in open dialog, show comfort in giving and receiving feedback, hold each other accountable, and demonstrate total commitment to their ongoing learning and development.

The coaching style of leadership needs reinforcement. Leaders at all levels must be recognized and rewarded for using coaching as their preferred style of leading and interacting with their teams. Therefore, coaching behaviors should be aligned and reflected in the performance assessment processes of the organization.

> To nurture a coaching culture, all the stakeholders must work collaboratively. Some organizations engage an external coaching body as a delivery partner to exchange ongoing feedback, ensuring continued growth and learning.

At the day's end, you don't want to build a coaching culture that diminishes in a few months. Following the five steps outlined above will increase the likelihood for the newly created coaching culture to last and extend.

Organizations with a strong coaching culture enjoy the greater rewards of having happy and satisfied employees, achieving bottom-line results, and retaining delighted customers in the longer run.

 **Nurturing a Speed Coaching Culture (Process & Tools)**

Nurturing a Speed Coaching Culture (Process & Tools)

Suppose we nosedive deeper into the organizations that have embraced coaching as a preferred leadership style. In that case, we will notice that coaching is a way of thinking, operating, interacting, and conversing daily for these companies. This coaching culture focuses on learning and development rather than simply achieving results.

A coaching culture is characterized by open communication, trust, and a willingness to learn from mistakes. In a coaching culture, everyone is encouraged to take responsibility for their own growth and to support the development of others.

With a strong coaching culture, managers and leaders act as coaches to help their employees develop their skills, identify areas for improvement, and achieve their goals. Teams are also encouraged to provide feedback to their colleagues and seek feedback for their own growth and development.

We have learned from these organizations that a coaching culture requires a safe environment where employees feel comfortable sharing their thoughts and feelings, trying new things, and making mistakes without fear of retribution. To make it happen, leadership commitment is the essential ingredient in building a coaching culture.

Top leaders need to be committed to creating and sustaining a coaching culture. This requires modeling coaching behavior, providing resources and training, and prioritizing coaching. I was stunned to see the ICF report about NASA's coaching intervention. NASA's investment in building a coaching culture led to a 21% increase in employee productivity, a 20% increase in employee satisfaction, and a 29% increase in leadership effectiveness.

As a coach-leader, you must communicate clear expectations around coaching like NASA. It would help if you clarified how it would be implemented, what it will look like in practice, and the benefits of coaching for the organization and individuals. Employees need to have opportunities to receive coaching, whether it's from their manager, peers, or external coaches. This can include formal coaching programs, regular check-ins, and ongoing feedback and support.

HOW TO SPOT A COACHING CULTURE?

Building a coaching culture is an advantageous investment. American Express, for instance, heavily invested in developing a coaching culture. They provided coaching skills training for their managers and employees, and the result was excellent. A study by the International Coach Federation found that the program increased employee productivity by 23%. The study also noticed a 19% increase in employee satisfaction and a 27% increase in leadership effectiveness.

You walk into an organization and would know whether or not they have a coaching culture. You will notice these signs in your interaction with teams and their leaders if you look carefully. You cannot help seeing them at IBM, for example. According to the ICF study, their coaching culture program led to a 60% increase in productivity and a 40% increase in employee satisfaction. IBM's leaders raised productivity by 70% due to enhanced leadership effectiveness.

Over the years, having helped several organizations embrace a coaching culture, I have observed seven critical signs indicating a strong coaching culture.

Sign #1: **Communication is open**

You can see open communication between employees and managers in a well-developed coaching culture. Employees feel comfortable sharing their thoughts and ideas, and managers are receptive to feedback.

Sign #2: **Everyone is accountable**

A coaching culture holds employees and managers accountable for their development and performance goals. There is a sense of shared responsibility for achieving these goals.

Sign #3: **People development is a priority**

A coaching culture prioritizes learning and development for all employees, and there are opportunities for growth and development at all levels of the organization.

Sign #4: **The work environment is positive**

A coaching culture creates a positive work environment where employees feel valued and supported. There is a sense of enthusiasm and energy around growth and development.

Sign #5: **Feedback is regular and continuous**

Regular and constructive feedback is a hallmark of a coaching culture. Employees receive feedback during formal performance reviews and also throughout the year.

Sign #6: **Collaboration is a norm**

A coaching culture encourages collaboration between employees and teams, fostering a sense of teamwork and shared success.

Sign #7: **Focus is on results**

A coaching culture is ultimately focused on achieving results. Organizations with a great coaching culture tend to see improved performance, higher employee engagement, and better business outcomes.

IDENTIFY THE CULTURE-KILLERS

The harsh truth is that organizations that fail to follow through on their coaching initiatives and integrate coaching into their ongoing operations struggle to establish a coaching culture that sticks.

Research and data can help organizations identify coaching culture challenges and develop effective strategies for overcoming them. In my experience, here are the top five elements that surely kill the coaching culture and cause the enormous investment in coaching to go down the drain.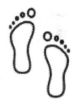

Killer #1: **Disinterested leaders:**

The top leadership's lack of support and commitment is the most devastating factor that becomes the major obstacle in developing a coaching culture. Leaders are expected to model coaching behaviors, but coaching culture wouldn't sustain when they don't.

Disinterested leaders fail to provide resources and necessary training to nurture the coaching culture. Coaching culture dies automatically when leaders don't prioritize coaching as essential to the organization's values and operations.

Killer #2: **Too much confusion:**

In many organizations, we have seen managers and their teams lose, and they do not understand what is expected of them in a coaching culture. Lack of clarity on goals, roles, and expectations makes building a thriving coaching culture difficult.

Killer #3: **Ineffective training:**

Last year, a top company invited us to rekindle the spark in their coaching culture. When my team and I dug deeper, we discovered that the managers and employees had not received adequate training to develop their coaching skills. The training they had received was conceptually wrong and had nothing to do with the actual concept, philosophy, and methodology of coaching. Managers were confused and clueless about applying the training concepts at the workplace.

I have learned through many similar examples that coaching remains ineffective or inconsistent without proper training and resources. Organizations that fail to provide their leader-coaches with the training they need to succeed struggle to establish a coaching culture.

Killer #4: **No accountability:**

A coaching culture requires accountability to ensure goals are met and development plans are followed. Coaching efforts will not lead to meaningful change or improvement without accountability.

For whatever reason, when companies do not provide clear goals and metrics for coaching effectiveness, it becomes difficult to measure the impact of coaching initiatives and hold Coaches and Coachees accountable for their performance.

Killer #5: **No measures:**

The old wisdom says, *'if you cannot measure it, you can't accomplish it.'* Many organizations lose momentum because they do not measure the impact of investment in coaching.

Most organizations struggle to measure the effectiveness of their coaching culture to make data-driven decisions and adjust their approach as necessary. Without effective measurement, it's difficult to determine whether coaching efforts have the desired impact.

I strongly recommend that as a coach-leader, you regularly take time out for the assessment and evaluation of energy, time, and resources invested in building a speed coaching culture. To me, this is the surest way for organizations to fine-tune their coaching strategies and maximize their impact.

PROCESS OF BUILDING A COACHING CULTURE

 Building a coaching culture is a huge undertaking, and it takes loads of effort. Talking is easy; doing is not. Your commitment as a leader will be the number one determining factor. Your ability to gain support from other leaders, bring them on board, and engage them in the process will be the key to success in this initiative.

More than process, it's the mindset behind the process that will generate impact. I am saying this not to demotivate you but to help you see the reality, eyeball to eyeball, and know precisely what you are signing up for. Building a coaching culture is a complex process requiring a comprehensive and thoughtful approach.

Here is a step-by-step process that we discovered through trial and error. It can be helpful for you too.

Step #1: **Assess**
Seeing precisely where you are and acknowledging it is a great way to build a coaching culture. Begin by assessing the organization's current culture.

How do you do it? By conducting surveys, focus groups, and interviews. This exercise will help you gain insight into the current culture, and you will know the strengths and areas for improvement in your organization's coaching culture.

Step #2: **Define**

What does a coaching culture mean to you? What does it mean to your organization? Are you considering adopting a coaching culture because everyone is talking about it or because you fully believe in it?

Develop a clear understanding of what behaviors, values, and attitudes will support a coaching culture.

Step #3: **Communicate**

Many coaching initiatives fail because they lack proper communication. Spend time developing a robust communication strategy. What message will you give, and how will it be delivered?

Proactively analyze how people might receive this message. Ensure you communicate the exact picture of a coaching culture you aim to build to everyone in the organization. Certify that everyone understands the benefits and what it means to them.

Step #4: **Enable**

Without managers having the skill to coach, the culture will not survive. What time, resources, and effort are you investing in building a coaching culture? You need to enable your teams with powerful coaching tools and processes.

Procter & Gamble (P&G) is an excellent example of enabling their teams with the skills and resources required for coaching. A case study published by the Harvard Business Review revealed that P&G's coaching culture program drastically improved employee engagement and productivity, reducing its turnover rate by 50%.

Whether you partner with an external coaching provider or do it yourself internally, make sure you design and deliver result-oriented training programs. Make sure you support your managers at all levels in developing the skills and knowledge to coach their teams effectively.

Google does it beautifully. Google is well-known for its coaching culture, which includes a formal coaching program for its managers. The program focuses on developing coaching skills and using feedback to support employee development. According to International Coach Federation, 88% of Google employees reported that their managers are effective coaches, and 79% said they would recommend Google as a pleasing workplace.

Step #5: **Encourage**

Feedback is the foundation of the entire coaching process. Find the proper method to facilitate feedback between employees and managers. Train your managers to make it safe for those on the receiving side of the input.

General Electric (GE) is a stunning example of encouraging its people to give and receive feedback. A case study published by the International Journal of Human Resource Management states that GE's coaching initiatives significantly improved employee performance and productivity. The company saw a return on investment of $1.5 million for every $1 million spent on coaching.

Learning from top organizations like GE, your job as a coaching leader is to create a culture of open communication and feedback. You must ensure employees and their managers feel comfortable exchanging a two-way feedback. You remove this safety, and you see the whole coaching culture collapsing.

Step #7: **Celebrate**

Celebrating success is necessary. It doesn't have to be a substantial big victory. It can only be a tiny achievement. Take time out to acknowledge and celebrate coaching behaviors. You may underestimate this statement, but remember; in my experience, celebrating these small victories gives your team the energy and confidence necessary to make coaching culture a preferred choice for everyone in the organization.

Combine some relevant rewards with celebrations. Recognizing employees and managers who demonstrate coaching behavior and mindset will be great. Leaders must take time to celebrate the success of those who apply the coaching style of leadership at the workplace. They also must identify and spotlight those who facilitate the development of a strong coaching culture.

Step #8: **Monitor**

You need to regularly evaluate the impact of the coaching culture through constant monitoring. There are metrics available, such as employee engagement, retention, and productivity, to assess the effectiveness of the coaching culture. Once you know where you are compared to where you want to be, you can adjust your approach and methods.

As I said earlier, building a coaching culture requires labor. It's painfully difficult. It requires sustained commitment, and it involves a top-down approach. It demands top leadership to set the tone for a coaching culture and provide support and resources to ensure the whole organization embraces the coaching culture.

WARNING SIGNS

Your entire effort in building the coaching culture can go to waste. I am seriously warning you.

Since you have come this far with me, I am sharing a few warning signs in this part of the book. If you keenly observe, you will notice these signs. These warning cyphers indicate that a coaching culture is slipping and that the investment in coaching is not producing the desired results. These signs can include:

Sign #1: **Lack of engagement:**
Employees not engaging in coaching conversations or seeking coaching opportunities could be a sign that the coaching culture is slipping. Lack of support from leadership or clarity around the benefits of coaching can cause this disengagement.

Sign #2: **Lack of investment:**
Another clear sign is when the organization is no longer investing in coaching or is cutting back on coaching resources. Of half a dozen organizations I witnessed pulling the plug on coaching investment, it was due to two reasons.
One, the top leadership was unaware of the perceived value of the coaching program.
Two, it was due to a lack of commitment to the coaching initiative.

Sign #3: **Disengaged Coaches**
When your pool of in-house coaches starts showing dissatisfaction with the coaching activities, it's a sign that the coaching culture is in danger. If coaches don't show excitement, stop contributing to the process, and withhold their ideas and effort, don't ignore these signs.
Lack of support or resources or clarity around the role of coaching in the organization can cause this disconnection.

Sign #4: **Low coaching effectiveness:**
If the coaching is not leading to improved performance, it could be a sign of vulnerable coaching culture. This could be due to a lack of coaching skills or a lack of focus on goals and metrics.

Sign #5: **Resistance to feedback:**

Suppose employees resist or are not using feedback to improve their performance. In that case, it could signify that the coaching culture is not effectively integrated into the organization's culture.

If these signs are present, it is necessary to reassess the coaching culture and make adjustments to ensure that it is appropriately integrated into the organization's culture and producing the desired results.

LEVELS OF BUILDING A COACHING CULTURE?

 Our research has identified four levels of building a coaching culture, and organizations can move from one level to another through intentional effort and continuous improvement. Here are four levels of creating a coaching culture, along with some ways in which organizations can move from one level to the next:

Level #1: **NO COACHING CULTURE**

In this stage, coaching is not a part of the organization's culture, and there is little or no emphasis on coaching as a development or performance improvement tool.

Organizations can start by introducing coaching concepts and techniques to leaders and employees to move from this level to the next. This can be done through training and development programs, coaching certifications, and coaching sessions with external coaches.

Companies should aim to create awareness and interest in coaching as a tool for development.

Level #2: **EMERGING COACHING CULTURE**

This stage is where coaching starts to be integrated into the organization's culture but is not yet fully embedded. Some coaching programs or initiatives may be in place, but they are not yet widespread or fully embraced by leaders and employees.

The reward of this will be phenomenal. Let me share a study by 'Coaching Culture at Work' about Tata Communications, revealing that the coaching culture program helped Tata to a 39% surge in employee productivity, a 29% increase in employee engagement, and a 53% rise in leadership effectiveness.

To move from this level to the next, like Tata Communications, organizations can expand the scope of coaching programs and initiatives and focus on building a coaching mindset among leaders and employees. Organizations can achieve this through initiatives like workshops, coaching circles, and coaching sessions with internal coaches.

Another example is the famous Southwest Airlines. It developed a robust coaching culture by providing coaching skills training for its managers. ICF found a 24% increase in employee engagement, a 20% growth in employee productivity, and a 33% rise in customer satisfaction.

As a coach-leader, your goal at this stage should be to create a sense of ownership and commitment to coaching among leaders and teams so that they, too, increase engagement and satisfaction for themselves and business results for the organization.

Level #3: **ESTABLISHED COACHING CULTURE**

Reaching this level means coaching is fully integrated into the organization's culture, and there is a widespread understanding and use of coaching as a tool for development and performance improvement. Coaching becomes a crucial part of the organization's talent development strategy. This stage is testament that you have successfully built a culture of continuous improvement and learning in your organization.

To move from this level to the next, organizations can focus on creating a coaching culture aligned with the organization's overall strategy and goals. Coaching assessments, coaching audits, and regular coaching programs and initiatives reviews can help companies do this.

This is the time to ensure that coaching fully integrates into the organization's DNA and drives the business success. For example, Google has a strong coaching culture, with leaders trained in coaching skills who use a coaching approach to manage their teams. The company also has a robust internal coaching program, where employees can receive coaching from trained coaches to help them develop their skills and achieve their goals.

Ayala Corporation, Philippines, was featured in a study by ICF for developing a strong coaching culture. Their coaching program produced a 31% increase in employee productivity, a 26% increase in employee satisfaction, and a 40% surge in leadership effectiveness.

Singapore Management University produced equally fascinating results through its investment in coaching culture. A case study by Coaching Culture at Work stated a 21% increase in employee productivity and a 17% upturn in employee satisfaction.

Level #4: **HIGH-PERFORMANCE COACHING CULTURE**
Here, coaching is not just a tool for development and performance improvement but a core part of the *organization's identity and competitive advantage.* Coaching is a critical component of the organization's success, and culture of high-performance coaching drives continuous improvement, innovation, and growth.

Starbucks, for instance, has a coaching culture that focuses on developing its employees and providing them with opportunities for growth and development. The company has a formal coaching program and a network of internal coaches who coach employees at all levels.

To maintain a high-performance coaching culture, organizations must continue to invest in coaching programs and initiatives and ensure that coaching is integrated into all aspects of the organization's strategy and operations. They must also cultivate a continuous learning and improvement culture and regularly assess and refine their coaching culture to align with the changing needs of the organization and its stakeholders.

The Royal Bank of Scotland (RBS), The Home Depot, JS Bank, McDonald's, Hilton Pharma, Allianz, Microsoft, PTCL (Pakistan) Hewlett-Packard, K-Electric (Pakistan), Infosys (India), DBS Bank (Singapore), Petronas (Malaysia), Bank Rakyat (Malaysia), GE, Descon Engineering, Kia Motors, P&G and Nestle are some of the top organizations I witnessed benefiting hugely by developing a Coaching Culture.

They witnessed significant improvements in employee productivity, engagement, satisfaction, and leadership effectiveness.

Data and evidence show that coaching culture can also reduce turnover rates, provide a massive return on investment for coaching efforts, and increase performance and productivity.

Examples of these organizations demonstrate that any organization can successfully develop a coaching culture by providing training and resources to support coaching, integrating coaching into leadership development programs, and creating a culture of accountability and continuous learning.

Are you ready to commit to a similar investment of time, effort, energy, and emotion to build a strong coaching culture in your organization?

Chapter 13

How do Coaching &
Routine Conversations Differ?

How do Coaching & Routine Conversations Differ?

Scores of conversations take place every day between a boss and their subordinates. Then what is so special about a coaching conversation? I call it *'impact.'* A coaching conversation triggers a different thinking and knowing process in the Coachee, influencing their ability to act differently.

A coaching conversation enables the Coachee to see things they have never seen before. Therefore, they chose to act; they had never performed before.

Let me give you a simple metaphor to help you understand the difference between ordinary and powerful coaching conversations. Do you know in what ways snorkeling and scuba diving are different?

The snorkeler swims at the surface, uses much energy to move, and thinks what he sees is beautiful. I don't discount the beautiful part, but he hasn't seen anything yet! He doesn't know what he's missing.

On the other hand, the scuba diver dives deep down, and she glides effortlessly underwater, almost like a fish. It's a different beautiful world she experiences down there, and she sees terrific things unseen to the people at the surface

Regular conversations are like snorkeling at the surface. You gather lots of *information*, but you exert a lot of energy. Coaching conversations are like scuba diving at the deep level. You make *discoveries*, and gain life-changing insights.

That is why coaching should be experienced and not merely explained by words. You can tell what scuba diving is to the snorkeler, but only to a certain extent; they have to experience it to see it for themselves.

My team and I have observed hundreds of routine and coaching conversations. Coaching conversations are entirely different in terms of their focus, outcomes, and environment in which they take place.

Coaching conversations are also called magical conversations. What makes those conversations so impactful and powerful? Seven key differences exist between a regular boss-subordinate interaction and a robust coach-Coachee conversation.

Difference #1: ARGUMENT-DRIVEN TALKING vs. UNDERSTANDING-DRIVEN LISTENING

This is the major shift. When managers embrace coaching, they talk less and listen more. They stop arguing with their direct reports and know that the conflict will only spoil the relationship.

Instead, they stay back and prefer to listen to their side of the story. While listening, they show understanding of their viewpoint without passing judgment.

Difference #2: HIGHLIGHTING MISTAKES vs. UNLEASHING STRENGTHS

Old-school managers were trained to spot mistakes. They had developed this unique eye to see the faults only. Not only were they good at catching flaws, but they were also brilliant at using those mistakes against their subordinates at the most appropriate time. This would give them a sense of power. However, it damages trust.

Coaching leaders, on the other hand, are strength-finders. They master the art of highlighting hidden gifts. Their direct reports feel better in their presence, and conversations automatically flow into solutions.

Difference #3: PROVING YOUR STANCE vs. PROVING YOUR COMMITMENT

When your direct reports bring problems to you, in the first few seconds of listening, you assume you have a perfect solution. You stop listening and start advising. However, your assumption is proving to be wrong. The other person still has valuable information to share that you should have encouraged them to speak out about. Without knowing the complete picture, you throw your solution that the other person is trying to push back.

This starts a debate. You both push your stance forward, proving that you are right. Your ego comes into play, and things get worse.

Coaching leaders know how to control their egos. Instead of thrusting their viewpoint and proving themselves right, they only make a sincere effort to prove they are there to provide full support. They never fail to convey this intent in the conversations that their direct reports can entirely rely on their support and guidance.

Difference #4: DEFENDING YOURSELF vs. SHOWING OPENNESS

Tons of energy is wasted daily in human interactions where each party is trying to safeguard itself. Coaching leaders understand that this self-defense is unnecessary. They bring openness to the conversation instead.

Their commitment to exploring varying perspectives enriches the conversation and leads to solutions no one had thought of before.

Difference #5: PROTECTING vs. VULNERABILITY

Now, this is a significant differentiator. In his book 'Culture Code' Denial Coyle has presented a key concept in building trust, *'vulnerability'*. When leaders show vulnerability, it binds them hard with their teams.

Coaching leaders rely on showing fragility as an alternative to protecting their position and viewpoint. They are fearless in exposing their weaker side to their teams. They eliminate their desire to be seen as a *'know it all'* type of person.

The cornerstone of establishing lasting respect, trust, and rapport is moving from protection to showing vulnerability.

Difference #6: MANIPULATING vs. COLLABORATING

 *'Command and control'* school of thought taught managers to be more controlling. They never waste a chance manipulating their team members and getting what they want.

However, teams feel being used and not valued. This constant control and manipulation damage the relationship. Direct reports constantly look for a chance to put the boss down and take revenge. In coaching conversations, managers operate from a position of collaboration and build trust, cooperation, and support through daily interactions.

Difference #7: DEMANDING CHANGE VS SUPPORTING CHANGE

Managers mostly show unhappiness with their teams. They want teams to change their behaviors, habits, or work style. Managers push people to change, and they demand it.

On the other hand, leaders who coach focus on ensuring their support to the people who choose to change. Their conversations do not threaten their direct reports, and people don't avoid those conversations.

Difference #8: LOCKED VS FLEXIBLE

In everyday conversations, leaders lock themselves in positions and standpoints, and this rigidity adds no value to the interaction. Conversations should not be seen as fixed stones; they should be viewed as moving water.

When leaders are locked in an immovable stance, dialogue becomes futile. No progress is made. People start hating interactions with their managers, and conversations become a burden.

Coaching leaders understand this reality. They unlock themselves and operate beyond positions and stances. They show flexibility to change their perspective when others seem more practical.

Difference #9: PAST VS FUTURE

Many routine conversations fail to produce the desired results because no matter how hard the person tries, the boss will pull the dialogue into the past. Past-centric conversations evoke defensiveness, guilt, and resentment. Moreover, these conversations produce no results. The dialogue doesn't move forward.

On the other hand, coaching conversations are focused on the future.  Coaching leaders know that digging too much into the past will achieve nothing. Keeping the discussion focused on the end outcome allows leaders to produce the desired impact.

At the end of every coaching conversation, you need to self-assess the quality of each interaction. Do you think the Coachee left the conversation energized, drained, or discouraged? Whether they feel energized or drained depends on many factors, including:

1. Did they feel respected?
2. Did they feel being fully heard?
3. Did they get a chance to defend their position?
4. Did they get a feeling that their opinion mattered?

Coaching conversations can create magic, and routine conversations can sometimes create disaster. What are you creating through your conversations with your team? I wish you magic.

Chapter 14

 Speed Coaching in Action

Speed Coaching in Action

In the last 20 years, I have had the privilege to run Executive Coaching and leadership development interventions with over 450 highly successful organizations in more than 40 countries. As a Leadership Coach, it was my most fantastic opportunity to work closely with hundreds of global industry leaders.

As a human behavior researcher, I developed an extraordinary curiosity for determining what makes leaders great. What makes them effective? What makes them deliver superior results consistently?

According to Michael Bungay Stanier, the author of the bestselling book 'Coaching Habit,' many coaching programs for leaders fail because of the following reasons:

1. Training programs are too theoretical, with little focus on coaching practice.
2. Training programs are entirely divorced from reality. Not relevant to the day-to-day challenges of busy executives.
3. Trainers fail to engage the executives. Participants feel bored and disconnected all through the learning process.

Working with thousands of leaders and executives in the last two decades, my team and I have collected loads of data to understand and address their challenges. Therefore, the concepts, tools, and frameworks I shared in this book represent and relate to the daily reality that busy executives face. Everything I brought into this book is totally practical. No fluff. No beating around the bush.

The book can replace a live training workshop's highly engaging learning experience. Therefore, I have tried making this book crisp, engaging, and fun.

 I have also experienced that although coaching training had all the elements that Michael Bungay Stanier pointed out, many executives we initially trained still fail to make coaching a daily practice. When we reconnected with them, we found out the following reasons:

1. After leaving the training program, they never spent time thinking or planning how to transfer this learning back to work.
2. They initially thought speed coaching would be easy. However, they discovered that the addiction to advice-giving is not easy to fight with. Not dictating and listening deeply seemed almost impossible.
3. They found that 'speed coaching' was slower comparing to problem-solving by offering a quick advice.
4. Also, they thought they lost control over their subordinates by not advising and appearing to have an answer to every problem.
5. When they learn to adopt the coaching mindset and combine it with a skillset, they begin to produce miracles in the lives of their teams.

Coaching Leaders allow people to experiment, find answers, and learn from their mistakes. Leaders quickly realize the benefit of this new style of engaging teams. Their traditional *'do as I say'* approach is replaced by *'what do you think?'*. They stop micromanaging. This one practice alone saves them plenty of time for the real leadership work they are actually hired for.

Managers need to figure out how many game-changing ideas they missed taking advantage of because they never considered asking their people for input. They loved being seen as the most competent person in the room. It never occurred to them that being the best in the room meant you were in the wrong room.

Coaching leaders enable employees to develop ideas that facilitate their intrinsic motivations. Research shows that when leaders use coaching, it improves employee motivation and performance and boosts satisfaction with both their job and their manager.

Many executives in our training confess that their previous knowledge and understanding about coaching was incorrect. They happily state that now they fully understand the core purpose, methodology, and process of coaching. One Executive shared his experience saying,

'I was having severe problems with my team. They needed to deliver on their commitments, and I was deeply concerned. I shared my worry with my boss, whose response was, *'just coach them'*. He did not bother asking me whether or not I was trained to coach. My boss has yet to offer me to attend any coaching training.

'Just coach them' is a popular but dangerous leadership approach. Because you never know what the person will do with their team in the name of coaching.

In our post-training reinforcement intervention, we observe leaders interacting with their teams at the workplace. We interview their direct reports about their leadership style.

Here are a few signs we spot when a leader puts speed coaching into action.

1. Leaders use appropriate questioning instead of prescribing solutions.

2. Leaders give constructive feedback instead of holding it.
3. In conversations, leaders take less air time and provide more chances for the other person to speak.
4. They listen carefully, effectively, and deeply.
5. Leaders use speed coaching to spot the team's strengths and actively work with the team to build them further.
6. Interactions are insightful. There is greater alignment between the two on both direction and action.
7. Leaders show more understanding of employees' viewpoints, perspectives, and opinions.
8. Direct reports leave the meeting motivated and energized instead of drained and stressed.

Coaching brings a transformation in leadership styles. We run a post-training assessment to see the impact of our *Speed Coaching* training. This includes interviews with participants, their direct reports, line manager, and peers. The results are always fascinating.

Our research with client organizations consistently reveals that coaching leaders become less concerned with telling others what, how, and when to complete a task. Instead, they empower their team members to discover solutions for themselves and act as leaders.

Another shift we notice is in their perception of their role. They learn to believe that their leadership is measured by their ability to inspire and influence their teams. They realize that nurturing talent and developing future leaders is one of the most critical measures of leadership impact.

For some leaders, making this transition is more complex than the others. The reason for this difficulty is their habit of getting things done alone. They have been accustomed to providing answers instead of asking. Waiting for the people to come up with the solution when they thought they know the best solution already, is a patience-requiring process. Their impulse to *tell* rather than *ask* is the primary obstacle in becoming effective coaching leaders.

Coach-like leaders discover that adopting a coaching style of leading is a game changer. They show excitement to run more coaching conversations and find coaching a real thought-provoking process. They love to engage their direct reports in conversations that help them improve their performance and overcome challenges independently.

Giving people a chance to utilize their abilities, skills, and knowledge to solve their problems is a significant change. A leader's ultimate wish would be to create an empowered team that can operate independently without relying too much on them for instructions. They wish to create a team where every member trusts their own knowledge, capability, and skill. Coaching makes this wish come true.

Although there are numerous skills a coaching leader can use when coaching their teams, leaders can use three essential techniques right away that will significantly impact how they engage with their teams, peers, and senior leadership.

PRACTICING SPEED COACHING OPPORTUNITIES

Situation #1:

An employee had a poor interaction with a customer on the phone. This was the third such impropriety by the employee this month.

Opportunity Missed: [Manager's Response]

- Provide corrective feedback or even punish the employee.

Opportunity Availed: [Coaching-Leader's Response]

- I've noticed this isn't your first challenging interaction with a customer lately. What do you see going on in these situations?

Situation #2

A colleague is having a conflict with one of her direct reports. They don't like each other and must work together. The colleague realizes she has been avoiding doing anything about this and that it's time for a discussion with the direct report, but she doesn't know where to begin. She asks for guidance.

Opportunity Missed: [Manager's Response]

- Advise the colleague with solutions and strategies to fix the problem.

Opportunity Availed: [Coaching-Leader's Response]

- What would a successful conversation with your direct report would look like? How would it go?

Situation #3

A direct report feels he is ready for a promotion. He is a decent performer but still needs to prepare for advancement. However, he is persistent and publicly shows dissatisfaction with management and the organization. The quality of his work has begun to slide as well.

Opportunity Missed: [Manager's Response]

- Temper the employee's behavior through direct confrontation or avoid and hope he leaves.

Opportunity Availed: [Coaching-Leader's Response]

- I understand your frustration with not getting promoted as quickly as you would like. Given the nature of the job you seek, what are your strengths and weaknesses in performing in that role today?

Situation #4

A teammate lacks life balance. She keeps long hours, feels burned out, and often has little resilience. She wants to improve her quality of life but needs to know how. She seeks your advice on what to do.

Opportunity Missed: [Manager's Response]

- Sympathize with the teammate, having not found great solutions for her overwork and stress.

Opportunity Availed: [Coaching-Leader's Response]

- What is quality life balance to you?

PRACTICING COACHING CONCEPTS

Here are some of the situations where managers have a chance to experiment with coaching skills:

1. When you assign tasks to your team members.
2. When you are supposed to give feedback to one of your direct reports.

3. When you are bringing new employees on board.
4. When your team member tries to give their monkeys away.
5. When you are helping others overcome setbacks or challenges.
6. When you are having a performance appraisal conversation.
7. When you deal with an employee having a performance problem.
8. When you want your direct reports to develop skills and abilities.
9. When you are creating a career path for your direct reports.
10. When you converse with an employee who has failed to do something "right."
11. When an employee wants help or guidance from you.
12. When your team members need a sounding board or want to vent

ALWAYS REMEMBER

1. A coach-like leader uses speed coaching to spot employees' strengths and actively works with the person to further build them.
2. Their interactions turn into insightful learning experiences.
3. There is greater alignment between the two of them on both direction *(what to do?)* and action *(when to do what?)*
4. Coach-like leaders show more understanding of employees' viewpoints, perspectives, and opinions.
5. After interacting with a coach-like leader, direct reports leave the interaction motivated and energized (instead of drained and stressed), making sure they turn insights into action and create impact.

YOUR KEY INSIGHTS & LEARNINGS
from Seed Coaching book

Following are the most powerful, heart-touching and practical insights I have learned, gathered, or reflected while reading Speed Coaching:

YOUR LEARNING APPLICATION PLAN
KNOWLEDGE INTO ACTION

This is my action plan to put into practice the mindset, skillset, framework and tools that I have learned in Speed Coaching:

REFERENCES

1. 'Brilliant Coaching' by Julie Starr. Peasrson Education Limited, 2017.
2. Study on Infosys: International Coach Federation. (2016). Building a Coaching Culture with 800 Leaders at Infosys.
3. "The Coaching Mindset: An 8-Step Approach to Navigating Your Way Through Change" by Tammy Holyfield
4. "The Leader's Guide to Coaching: Discovering the Power of Listening and Learning" by Marlene Chism
5. "The Future of Coaching: Vision, Leadership and Responsibility in a Transforming World" edited by Hetty Einzig
6. "Transformational Coaching: Shifting Mindsets for Sustainable Change" by Richard Enlow
7. "The Conscious Coach: Powerful Tools to Transform Your Coaching Practice" by Mark Matousek
8. Case study on IndusInd Bank: Coaching Culture at Work. (2017). IndusInd Bank: Creating a Coaching Culture.
9. Case study on DBS Bank: Coaching Culture at Work. (2017). DBS Bank: Making Coaching a Core Leadership Competency.
10. Study on Petronas: International Coach Federation. (2014). Coaching for Improved Work Performance: The Effect of Executive Coaching on Work Performance.
11. Case study on Bank Rakyat: Coaching Culture at Work. (2017). Bank Rakyat: Creating a Coaching Culture to Drive Performance and Engagement.
12. Case study on Wipro: Coaching Culture at Work. (2017). Wipro: Developing a Coaching Culture to Drive Business Results.

13. Study on HCL Technologies: International Coach Federation. (2016). A Research Study of the Effectiveness of Internal Coaching in HCL Technologies.

14. Case study on Singapore Management University:

15. Coaching Culture at Work. (2017). Singapore Management University: Developing a Coaching Culture to Improve Performance.

16. Case study on Tata Communications: Coaching Culture at Work. (2017).

17. Study on Ayala Corporation: International Coach Federation. (2017). The Impact of Executive Coaching on Performance: The Ayala Corporation Experience.

18. "Co-Active Coaching: The Proven Framework for Transformative Conversations at Work and in Life" by Henry Kimsey-House, Karen Kimsey-House, Phillip Sandahl, and Laura Whitworth

19. "The Mindful Coach: Seven Roles for Helping People Grow" by Doug Silsbee

20. "Leadership Coaching: The Disciplines, Skills and Heart of a Coach" by Tony Stoltzfus

21. "The Art of Possibility: Transforming Professional and Personal Life" by Rosamund Stone Zander and Benjamin Zander

22. "The Coaching Habit: Say Less, Ask More & Change the Way You Lead Forever" by Michael Bungay Stanier

23. "Executive Coaching with Backbone and Heart: A Systems Approach to Engaging Leaders with Their Challenges" by Mary Beth O'Neill

24. "Becoming an Exceptional Executive Coach: Use Your Knowledge, Experience, and Intuition to Help Leaders Excel" by Michael Frisch and Robert Lee

25. "The Tao of Coaching: Boost Your Effectiveness at Work by Inspiring and Developing Those Around You" by Max Landsberg

26. "On Becoming a Leadership Coach: A Holistic Approach to Coaching Excellence" by Christine Wahl and Clarice Scriber

27. "The Coaches' Handbook: Eight Steps to Success" by Sarah Cook

28. "The Art of Coaching Teams: Building Resilient Communities that Transform Schools" by Elena Aguilar

29. "The Essential Guide to Business Coaching" by Elaine Cox and Tatiana Bachkirova

30. "Coaching for Performance: The Principles and Practice of Coaching and Leadership" by John Whitmore

31. "The Coaching Connection: A Manager's Guide to Developing Individual Potential in the Context of the Organization" by John Hoover and Paul J. Gorrell

32. "Executive Coaching for Results: The Definitive Guide to Developing Organizational Leaders" by Brian O. Underhill, Kimcee McAnally, and John Koriath

33. "The Elements of Mentoring" by W. Brad Johnson and Charles R. Ridley

34. "The Leader as Coach: Strategies for Coaching and Developing Others" by David B. Peterson

35. "Coaching Questions: A Coach's Guide to Powerful Asking Skills" by Tony Stoltzfus

36. "The Power of Resilience: Achieving Balance, Confidence, and Personal Strength in Your Life" by Robert Brooks and Sam Goldstein

37. "Mastering Executive Coaching: Theory and Practice of Leading Successful Coaching Engagements" by Sabine Dembkowski, Fiona Eldridge, and Ian Hunter

38. "The Coaching Manager: Developing Top Talent in Business" by James M. Hunt and Joseph R. Weintraub

39. 'The Coaching Manual' by Julie Starr, 2015.

40. "Leadership Coaching: Working with Leaders to Develop Elite Performance" by Jonathan Passmore and Brian Underhill

41. "Leaders as Teachers: Unlock the Teaching Potential of Your Company's Best and Brightest" by Ed Betof and Laurie Bassi

42. "The Leader's Guide to Coaching & Mentoring: How to Use Soft Skills to Get Hard Results" by Mike Brent and Fiona Dent

43. "Coaching for Leadership: The Practice of Leadership Coaching from the World's Greatest Coaches" by Marshall Goldsmith, Laurence Lyons, and Sarah McArthur

44. "Coaching for Leadership: Writings on Leadership from the World's Greatest Coaches" by Marshall Goldsmith, Laurence Lyons, and Sarah McArthur

45. "Executive Coaching: A Guide for the HR Professional" by Anna-Marie Richard

46. "Coaching Skills for Leaders in the Workplace: How to Develop, Motivate and Get the Best from Your Staff" by Jackie Arnold

47. "The Coach's Casebook: Mastering the Twelve Traits That Trap Us" by Geoff Watts

48. "The Coaching Mindset: 8 Ways to Think Like a Coach" by Chad Hall and Bill Copper

49. "The Leadership Coach's Playbook: Creating a Winning Team" by Nathan Regier

50. "The Leader as Coach: Developing Coaching Skills for Success" by Karen Tweedie

51. "Team Coaching with the Solution Circle: A Practical Guide to Solution Focused Team Development" by Daniel Meier and Christoph Meier

52. "Leadership Coaching: The Definitive Guide to Executive Coaching and Leadership Development" by Jonathan Passmore and Nick Nairn

53. "The Seven Habits of Highly Effective Coaches" by Michael Bungay Stanier (Harvard Business Review)

54. "The Case for Executive Coaching" by James Hunt and Joseph Weintraub (Harvard Business Review)

55. "How Leaders Become Self-Aware" by Anthony K. Tjan (Harvard Business Review)

56. "Leadership Coaching: Why Coach, What to Look For, How to Choose" by Gary Ranker (Forbes)

57. "10 Keys to Successful Executive Coaching" by Jeff Gothelf (Entrepreneur)

58. "The Impact of Executive Coaching and 360-Degree Feedback on Leadership Effectiveness" by Laura S. Page and Kurt W. Conrad (Journal of Leadership and Organizational Studies)

59. "The Leadership Coaching Guide" by Jennifer Porter (Harvard Business Review)

60. "The Four Biggest Myths about Executive Coaching" by Deborah Grayson Riegel (Harvard Business Review)

61. "How Coaching Can Help a Leader Grow" by John Baldoni (Harvard Business Review)

62. "The Art of Leadership Coaching: Why It Works and How to Do It" by Jay A. Conger (Organizational Dynamics)

63. "The Leader as Coach" by Marshall Goldsmith (Harvard Business Review)

64. "Developing a Coaching Mindset" by Sarah Green Carmichael (Harvard Business Review)

65. "The Benefits of a Coach-Like Approach to Leadership" by Michael Bungay Stanier (Fast Company)

66. "Why Leaders Should Act More Like Professional Coaches" by Liz Kislik (Harvard Business Review)

67. "The Coaching Leader: A Model for Our Times" by David A. Kolb (Organizational Dynamics)

68. "Becoming a Coach-Like Leader" by John Hillen and Mark Nevins (Harvard Business Review)

69. "Creating a Coaching Culture" by David Peterson (Strategy + Business)

70. "How to Develop Your Coaching Skills" by Jennifer Porter (Harvard Business Review)

71. "The Coach-Like Leader: Make the Transition from Managing to Coaching" by Bob Dusin and Susan Stautberg (Leadership Excellence)
72. "What Does It Mean to Be a 'Coach-Like' Leader?" by Doug Ringer (Forbes)
73. "The Art of Coaching" by Tara Sophia Mohr (Harvard Business Review)
74. "Coaching for Engagement" by Annie McKee (Harvard Business Review)
75. "Becoming a More Coach-Like Leader" by Kristi Hedges (Forbes)
76. "Leading Through Coaching: Unlocking Potential in Others and Ourselves" by Jacqueline Carter (Linkage)
77. "From Boss to Coach: The Manager's Guide to Coaching Employees" by Diane Coutu and Carol Kauffman (Harvard Business Review)
78. "Becoming a Coach-Like Leader: What Every CEO Should Know" by Mark S. Babbitt (Inc.)
79. "The Art of the Coaching Conversation" by Jennifer Porter (Harvard Business Review)
80. "Coaching Can Make a Difference: Tips for Being an Effective Coach" by Art Petty (Forbes)
81. "Why Leaders Need to Be Coaches, Not Bosses" by Rachel Feintzeig (The Wall Street Journal)
82. "The Mindset of a Coaching Leader" by Michael Bungay Stanier (Harvard Business Review)
83. https://work.chron.com/coach-management-vs-boss-management-style-20551.html
84. https://www.businessnewsdaily.com/10541-coach-not-boss.html
85. https://futureofworking.com/15-advantages-and-disadvantages-of-the-authoritarian-leadership-style/
86. https://www.businessnewsdaily.com/10541-coach-not-boss.html

87. https://www.worksmartpeo.com/4-tips-making-transition-manager-coach/

88. The Coaching Habit_ Say, Less, Ask More & Change the Way You Lead Forever, Michael Bungay Stanier

89. Why is workplace development important to a company's well-being?. https://www.linkedin.com/pulse/why-workplace-development-important-companys-well-being-

90. Anti Microbial Qualities of Copper | Kaarigar Handicrafts Inc.. https://kaarigarhandicrafts.com/blogs/kaarigar/anti-microbial-qualities-of-copper

91. https://www.beckershospitalreview.com/patient-safety-outcomes/some-hospital-staff-confuse-emergency-codes-study-finds.html

92. Cullison, Andrew. "Next Level Employees Need Next Level Leaders." Indianapolis Business Journal, vol. 40, no. 23, IBJ Corporation, Aug. 2019, p. 13.

93. Why is workplace development important to a company's well-being?. https://www.linkedin.com/pulse/why-workplace-development-important-companys-well-being-

94. Leadership Courses - Big Think+. https://bigthink.com/plus/capabilities/leadership-courses/

95. Why is workplace development important to a company's well-being?. https://www.linkedin.com/pulse/why-workplace-development-important-companys-well-being-

96. Cullison, Andrew. "Next Level Employees Need Next Level Leaders." Indianapolis Business Journal, vol. 40, no. 23, IBJ Corporation, Aug. 2019, p. 13.

97. Why is workplace development important to a company's well-being?. https://www.linkedin.com/pulse/why-workplace-development-important-companys-well-being-

98. PSYCHOLOGICAL SAFETY. zhttps://www.linkedin.com/pulse/psychological-safety-innocent-ociti/

99. Deputy Manager Interview Questions And Answers-ZigsawBlog.https://www.zigsaw.in/jobs/deputy-manager-interview-questions-and-answers/

100. Conor Cudahy's work in Malawi ended abruptly because of COVID. Now he's https://www.bostonglobe.com/2023/01/24/l

101. Sincere Heart Touching Love Messages For Your Sweetheart. http://lovemessagesfromheart.com/sincere-heart-touching-love-messages-for-your-sweetheart/

102. Coaching for Breakthrough (2013), Peter Chee

103. Coaching with Spirit (2003), Teri .E Belf

104. Super Coach (2009), Michael Neil

105. The Power of Appreciation (2003), Noella, C, Nelson

106. The Infinite Games, (2019), Simon Sinek

107. Hausenblas, Heather. "Where We Live Could Affect Efforts to Live a Healthier Life." Florida Times Union, Florida Times Union, 1 Feb. 2016, p. D.1.

108. Arush Thapar på LinkedIn: CASE STUDY: GENERATING LEADS FOR A RENOWNED .... https://se.linkedin.com/posts/arush-thapar_case-study-generating-leads-for-a-renowned-activity-7023281989977792512-atMY

109. Why Is Respect Important? (19 Reasons) - Enlightio. https://enlightio.com/why-is-respect-important

110. Cullison, Andrew. "Next Level Employees Need Next Level Leaders." Indianapolis Business Journal, vol. 40, no. 23, IBJ Corporation, Aug. 2019, p. 13.

111. 7 Steps to Learn from Mistakes and Grow as a Person - Develop Good Habits. https://www.developgoodhabits.com/learn-mistakes/

112. https://work.chron.com/coach-management-vs-boss-management-style-20551.html

113. https://www.businessnewsdaily.com/10541-coach-not-boss.html

114. https://futureofworking.com/15-advantages-and-disadvantages-of-the-authoritarian-leadership-style/

115. Stealth Coaching: Everyday Conversations for Extraordinary Results. By Rob Kramer – January 23, 2013

116. https://www.strengthscope.com/common-barriers-coaching-culture-overcome/

117. https://www.xponents.com/resources/white-pages-and-articles/3-barriers-implementing-coaching-culture-overcome

118. Trust Factor: The Science of Creating High-Performance Culture, (2017) Paul Zak

119. 12 Rules of Life: An antidote to Choas, (2018) Jordan Peterson

120. Whom can you Trust: How Technology has Brought Us Together and Why it Might Drive Us Apart, (2018) Rachel Botsma

121. Work is Love, Made it Visible (2018), Marshall Goldsmith

122. Leadershift: The 11 Essential Changes Every Leader Must Embrace. John C. Maxwell

123. Coaching at work, 2007, powering your team with awareness, responsibility, and trust, Matt Somers, Page # 74

124. Coaching at work, 2007, powering your team with

125. understanding, commitment, and trust, Matt Somers, Page # 74

126. Work is Love, Made it Visible (2018), Marshall Goldsmith

127. Leadershift: The 11 Essential Changes Every Leader Must Embrace. John C. Maxwell

128. A playbook for finding the ideal employee | TED Talks. https://www.ted.com/playlists/500/talks to help you find the ide

129. "Sound Bites." Journal of Property Management, vol. 82, no. 1, Institute of Real Estate Management, Jan. 2017, p. 5.

130. Love Actually (2003) - Emma Thompson as Karen-IMDb.https://www.imdb.com/title/tt0314331/characters/nm0000668

ACKNOWLEDGMENTS

- My heartfelt gratitude to my guru, **Dr. Marshall Goldsmith,** for showing up in my life as the most powerful and kindest teacher I have ever had. I have not seen anyone else in the global learning industry as generous as Marshall. Your unparalleled commitment to going the extra mile to help your students grow and progress is simply phenomenal.

- A big, wholehearted thank you to my mentor, my brother, **Arif Anis**, for being an unstoppable source of inspiration for me in the last two decades. From being my first coach to becoming my guide to putting my work on the international map, you have been my most reliable, rock-solid support.

- My sincerest appreciation to my guru, **Will Linssen**, for opening so many doors of possibilities for me. Your guidance and mentoring have made a massive difference in my life.

- My earnest recognition for the legend, **Dave Ulrich**, for always role-modeling for me with the highest level of professionalism, humility, and responsiveness. The day I became your mentee, my life changed to a whole new level.

- I wholeheartedly appreciate and thank the legendary coach-maker **Julie Starr**, for reinforcing and shaping my coaching concepts. Your books and guidance have helped me become a better Coach and transform many coaches through my coach-education initiatives.

- My heartiest thanks to my Son, **Hussain Abbas**, who is my best friend also. Thank you, Hussain, for filling my life with your purest love and challenging my coaching philosophy and methods through your power questions. You are my most trustworthy partner in practicing coaching in our daily conversations.

- Thank you, **Rashda Abbas**, for being a great life partner and a continued source of peace and fulfillment in my life. Your professional success journey is a significant source of motivation and inspiration for millions of young girls across the globe.
- Thank you, **Team Possibilities**, for allowing me to write and for undertaking massive coaching research projects in the last many years.

Some of my professional colleagues and friends deserve a specific mention.

I would like to give special credit to Arif Anis, Masood Ali Khan, Dr. Saima Ghazal, Sabeen Khalid, Hira Lal Bharvani, Shoaib Baig, Usman Abid, Ashaar Saeed, Shan Ashray, Fozia Masood, Asif Rizvi, Syed Zulfiqar Ali, Maqsood Ali, Omar Farooq, Syed Moonis Alvi, Rizwan Ali Shah, Muhammad Ijaz, Anwar Ul Haq, Shafaat Hashmi, Bakhtiar Khawaja, Rizwan Dalia, and Oana Alexandra, for constantly supporting and challenging my ideas, projects and initiatives.

LEADERSHIP COACHING

ONE-ON-ONE PRIVATE EXPERIENCE

Coaching can be a game-changer for leaders in challenging times for individual growth and organizational success. Qaiser is helping leaders produce transformational results for themselves and their organizations and communities, especially to succeed in a post-Covid world.

Qaiser will take your leaders through a yearlong coaching journey helping them make measurable changes in their leadership effectiveness and behavior.

To engage Qaiser and his Team of over 300 Certified Global Coaches spread over four continents for a leadership coaching experience for yourself, your CEO, and other Senior Leaders in your organization, please write at info@possibilitiesglobal.com

SPEED COACHING TRAINING

COACHING SKILLS TRAINING FOR LEADERS

Organizations constantly engage Qaiser Abbas and his team of Coaches, Coach-educators, and Trainers to teach Coaching Skills to their leaders and people managers across the organization.

Through our well-structured programs (based on pre-training assessment, post-training workplace application support, and follow-up on coaching skills ROI process), we are helping hundreds of organizations worldwide to build a coaching culture.

To engage Qaiser and his Team for training on the Coaching Style of Leadership, please write at info@possibilitiesglobal.com

Organizations may also approach our team to help them build an in-house team of coaches.

KEYNOTE SPEAKING

CONFERENCES, STRATEGY & BUSINESS MEETINGS

Qaiser Abbas is one of the most sought-after keynote speakers. The organizations regularly invite him to speak at their Annual Business Conferences, Strategic Retreats, Sales Meetups, and Awaydays. These sessions range from 30-minute power talks to full-day offsite sessions.

These talks are fun-filled, mind-shaking, and action-driven learning experiences that inspire and empower leaders and their teams to face market challenges and deliver results. Qaiser will also help you measure your return on investment made in developing your people.

To invite Qaiser or his team of over 100 senior trainers and speakers for a power-packed keynote session anywhere in the world, please write at info@possibilitiesglobal.com

Printed in the United States
by Baker & Taylor Publisher Services